TAME THE DIGITAL CHAOS

DISTRACTION, TIME, TASK & EMAIL MANAGEMENT IN AN AGE OF INFORMATION OVERLOAD

Paul J. Unger, Esq.

© 2021 Paul J. Unger, Esq.

ISBN: 978-0-578-84136-6

All rights reserved. No portion of this book may be reproduced without express written permission of the author.

For reproduction permission, contact:

Paul J. Unger, Esq.
punger@affinityconsulting.com
www.pauljunger.com or www.affinityconsulting.com

The following trademarks appear throughout this book: Microsoft, Windows, Windows 10, Microsoft Office, Microsoft 365, Microsoft SharePoint, Microsoft Outlook, Microsoft OneNote, Microsoft ToDo, Apple, iPad, NetDocuments, Worldox, iManage, Centerbase, Clio, PracticeMaster, Actionstep, LawBase, RocketMatter, Asana, OmniFocus, Todoist, GoodNotes, Pomodoro Technique, Getting Things Done, GTD, Google, Gmail, Five Dysfunctions of a Team, The Infinite Game, Zoom, GoToMeeting, The One-Minute Manager, TextExpander, Fujitsi ScanSnap, and Fritos.

MEET THE AUTHOR

Paul J. Unger, Esq.

Paul J. Unger is a nationally-recognized speaker, author, and thought-leader in the legal technology industry. He is an attorney and founding principal of Affinity Consulting Group, a nationwide consulting company providing legal technology consulting, continuing legal education, and training. He is the author of dozens legal technology manuals and publications, including recently published books *Fight the Paper* (2019) and *PowerPoint in an Hour for Lawyers* (2014). He served as Chair of the ABA Legal Technology Resource Center (2012-13, 2013-14) (www.lawtechnology.org) and Chair of ABA TECHSHOW (2011) (www.techshow.com). Mr. Unger now spends most of his time speaking, coaching, leading professional development programs for lawyers, and conducting technology and practice management assessments.

Table of Contents

Introduction 1

Chapter 1.

Distraction Management

Pardon the Interruption 3
    Self-Assessment 3
Information Overload—Distractions and the Cost of
Task-Switching 4
    Attention Deficit Trait 5
    Personal Health 6
    Workplace or Organizational Health 6
    Learn a Time, Task, and Email Management Methodology .. 7
    Attention Management Strategies 7
    Digital Detox—A Balanced Approach 12

Chapter 2.

Email Management

The Email Problem 15
Methodology to Conquer Email—Your Game Plan 16
    Reduce the Number of Emails You Receive 16
    Process Emails Faster and More Efficiently with Templates
        or AutoText Entries 18
    Allow a Trusted Assistant to Help Process Your Email 21
    Batch Process Emails 22
    Touch the Email One Time + 3-Minute Rule 23
    Delete, Do, Delegate, and Delay 24
    Delete 25
    Do—Just Resolve it! 27
    Delegate 28
    Delay—If Necessary 30
    Treat Your Email Inbox Like Your U.S. Mailbox at Home—
        Clear it Daily! 36

CHAPTER 3.

TASK AND DEADLINE MANAGEMENT

THE "TASK" PROBLEM 38
THE PROCESS 39
    Capture Tasks and Deadlines—Step One 40
    Gathering and Getting Organized—Step Two 41
    Review and Revision – Weekly Deep Dive—Step Three 50
    Planning Your Daily & Weekly Roadmap—Step Four 50
    Execution—Step Five 51
    Summary 51

CHAPTER 4.

TASKS—THE RIGHT TOOL TO MANAGE TASKS

PAPER OR SOFTWARE? 53
    Why Digital Task Lists Failed You in the Past 53
    Why Software is Better than Paper for Your Master Task List 54
OUTLOOK TASKS AND MICROSOFT TODO 55
    Task Folders 56
    Creating a Task in Outlook 62
    Creating a Task in Microsoft ToDo 64
    Microsoft ToDo—Everywhere 67
OTHER AVAILABLE PROGRAMS AND APPS 68
    Other Task Lists 68

CHAPTER 5.

TASK MANAGEMENT—DAILY PLANNING

HOW TO CREATE YOUR DAILY PLAN 70
    The Simple Index Card 70
    Tame the Digital Chaos Daily Planning Journal 71
    Using your iPad or Tablet 73
    Microsoft ToDo—My Day 74

CHAPTER 6.

TASK MANAGEMENT—WEEKLY PLANNING

HOW TO DO A WEEKLY DEEP DIVE 76

CHAPTER 7.

OUTLOOK ESSENTIALS FOR BETTER TIME, TASK, AND EMAIL MANAGEMENT

INTRODUCTION 83
INBOX TOOLS FOR BETTER ORGANIZATION 83
   Storage and Organization Problems with Email 83
   Set Up Folders to Organize Your Inbox 84
   Outlook Rule—Auto Route Email to Subfolder 86
   Outlook Rule—Notify Me of Emails from Very Important
      People (VIPs) 87
   Outlook Rule—Delay Delivery by 1 Minute 88
   Outlook Rules—Managing, Editing, Deleting, Turning On
      or Off 89
   Conditional Formatting to Apply Colors to Special Emails 90
   Flagging Email 92
   Outlook Views 94
   Out of Office Assistant 95
   Signatures 96
   Archiving Email 98
   Quick Steps 99

CHAPTER 8.

THE "NOT TO-DO LIST" - YOUR 26 WEEK PLAN

   Week 1 - Do NOT Neglect Sleep! 102
   Week 2 - Do NOT Worry So Much! 104
   Week 3 – Do NOT Doomscroll or Doomsurf 105
   Week 4 - Do NOT Ruminate – Learn to Tame "Monkey
      Mind" 106
   Week 5 - Do NOT Go Without Deep Breathing 108
   Week 6 - Do NOT Neglect Your Brain by Feeding it Poor
      Nutrition 108
   Week 7 - Do NOT Begin Your Day Without a Plan 109

Week 8 - Do NOT Start Your Day Without a Team Huddle 110
Week 9 - Do NOT Begin Your Week Without Weekly Planning 111
Week 10 - Do NOT Fail to Write Down Tasks and Random Neural Firings 111
Week 11 - Do NOT Keep 20 Different Lists 112
Week 12 - Do NOT Use Poor Descriptions in Your Task Lists! 113
Week 13 - Do NOT Underutilize Your Calendar 114
Week 14 - Do NOT Keep Your Outlook Inbox Up on Your Computer Monitor All Day 115
Week 15 - Do NOT Turn on Notifications 116
Week 16 - Do NOT Answer All Calls as They Come In ... 117
Week 17 - Do NOT Multitask! 117
Week 18 – Do NOT Juggle Tasks Without Some Juggling Tools 118
Week 19 - Do NOT Carry Your Phone 24/7 120
Week 20 - Do NOT Live on Social Media 24/7 121
Week 21 —Do NOT Micro-Manage and Solve Everyone's Problems! 121
Week 22 - Do NOT Create More Emails for Yourself 122
Week 23 - Do NOT Process Emails All by Yourself 123
Week 24 - Do NOT Do Shallow Work First Thing in the Morning 124
Week 25 - Do NOT Neglect Adequate Training 124
Week 26 - Do NOT Maintain a Paper File! Fight the Paper 125

CHAPTER 9.

APPENDIX—TDC DAILY PLANNER

Introduction

The Problem with Time in the Age of "Infomania"

The goal of this book is simple—to teach you time and task management skills and to help you cultivate the habits you need to make technology your servant so that you can regain control of your workday and personal life.

Technology is supposed to be our servant. However, for most of us, we have become a servant to technology. We need to turn that scenario around, and make technology work for us, not against us. Technology is supposed to be helping us do more in less time, but instead, it is controlling us in a very negative way. You've heard it— do more in less time and go home early, right? What happened to that? In my humble opinion, we have done the opposite. We have all become so dazzled by technology that we have lost all common sense. I hear comments all the time like:

"I can't get anything done because I get so many emails every day!"

"My work piles up because of all my interruptions."

"I do better with good old-fashioned paper."

"I can't keep track of my tasks . . . I constantly let things slip between the cracks."

Managing tasks and time is a problem that has been around for centuries. Most of us wish that we had another few hours a day to get things done. For most of us, technology has hurt us almost as much as it has helped us. With all the emails, instant messages, smartphones, social media posts, laptop computers, and tablets, we cannot escape the endless number of interruptions that prevent us from focusing and "being present" to tackle all that we must do every single day.

To compound the problem, most professionals are a digital mess! To achieve effective time, document, and email management, we must "get organized." To be organized today, we absolutely must figure out how to manage digital information. According to one study, we receive via digital delivery (email, text, and social media on our phones, computers, etc.), the equivalent of 140 newspapers of information per day. This can be overwhelming, especially if you do not have a system in place to process that digital information.

As one example, approximately 1 attorney in 10 have eliminated over 90% of paper files. In other words, only 1 in 10 have stopped maintaining a paper file and rely solely on a digital file. Quite frankly, this is terrible.

The good news is that the tools necessary to eliminate paper are available, easy to use, and inexpensive. Of course, this hasn't always been the case. Back in the '90s, scanners were very expensive and relatively slow. Document management systems weren't very easy to use, and they were also expensive and made primarily for large organizations. Electronic storage space on servers was also expensive. Since that time, the tools have steadily improved as their costs have declined. Secure cloud storage is a highly competitive market, and therefore, there are many solutions available at a reasonable cost. As a result, the benefits of paper reduction now far outweigh the costs of implementing such a system.

The methodologies outlined in this book combines distraction management skills, digital information strategies, with proven time management techniques utilizing technology tools for professionals in a practical and simple way. Many time management experts shy away from technology. I firmly believe this is a huge mistake. We must find a balance! Reverting to paper in today's modern world is a cop-out, especially in the age of technology and smartphones.

Chapter 1.

DISTRACTION MANAGEMENT

PARDON THE INTERRUPTION

In an eight-hour workday, if we receive 100 emails, that equates to receiving one email every 4.8 minutes. Combine that with instant messages, phone calls, and email curiosity breaks, and that equates to an interruption about every 2–3 minutes! Sound familiar? Let's assess your situation.

Self-Assessment

Take the following quick survey (analyze your daily average). How many of the following do you receive on a daily basis?

- Emails: _____

- Instant messages: _____

- Phone calls: _____

- Internet curiosity breaks: _____

- Total Interruptions: _____

- Divide your total into 480:_____
  (interruption every this many minutes) _____

  Other important questions:

- Identify the people (generally) you must respond to immediately. _____

- Identify the people (generally) you must respond to within 2 hours. _____

- Identify the people (generally) you can respond to by the end of the day. _____

- Identify the people (generally) you can respond to within 1-2 days. _____

- Do you and your team members give each other some uninterrupted time? _____

- Has technology simplified your life? _____

- Do you feel technology is controlling you? _____

INFORMATION OVERLOAD— DISTRACTIONS AND THE COST OF TASK-SWITCHING

150 emails, 50 instant messages, 20 telephone calls, 15 walk-in interruptions, 25 social media notifications, 50 email or internet curiosity breaks—that totals 310 digital interruptions. Divide that into 480 workday minutes and that is an interruption every 1.55 minutes.

Most studies indicate that the average professional is interrupted every 2–3 minutes. Now let's look specifically at just internal interruptions. The average worker checks Facebook 21 times per day, takes 74 email curiosity breaks, and switches tasks on a computer 564 times a day. With these numbers of external and internal interruptions, it is incredible that we get any deep level project work accomplished.

In a 2007 Microsoft study, researchers concluded that it takes 15-minutes to return to the work that computer programmers were performing at the time of an electronic-based interruption. If we get interrupted every 2–3 minutes and it takes 15 minutes to return to the work we were performing, how do we get anything done during the day? To make matters worse, most post-2015 studies indicate that it now takes 23 minutes to return to the task that we were performing before an interruption, and 40% never return to that task after dealing with the interruption. This is why we look at our timesheets somedays at 5 pm and see only 2 hours of billable time but it feels like we put in a 14-hour day.

Attention Deficit Trait

The reality is that we live in an age of information overload. We are constantly connected to the world and inundated with information. We sleep with our smartphones, we are surrounded by 24-hour news networks, add in social media and tablet computers—we can't escape. This is why very smart people underperform. Do you ever wonder why your head is in a constant cloud and you are unable to focus? It is called Attention Deficit Trait (ADT) and it is a world-wide epidemic.

ADT is a relative to Attention Deficit Disorder (ADD), but it is very different in that ADD has a genetic component; ADT does not. ADT is environmentally induced, and in today's age of information overload, those environmental factors are technology-based. In other words, ADT is a condition that is in large part caused by technology and the connectivity that we love so much. Yes, the very technology that we love so much is causing us to walk around like zombies. The scary part is that no one knows the long-term effects of information overload. However, some studies suggest that the problem is getting worse.

What can we do about it? We need to rethink and realign the way that our lives intersect with technology. Listen, I love technology. It is my life and passion, but sometimes it is frustrating, especially when it has a negative impact on productivity and my personal life. We combat ADT and overcome our inability to focus by attacking ADT on four fronts:

1. Enhancing our personal health,

2. Building our workplace health,

3. Learning a time, task, and email methodology, and

4. Acquiring attention and distraction management skills.

Personal Health

Personal health includes both physical and mental health. I am not an expert on this topic, and it is not the focus of this book, but it is important enough to mention when discussing gaining control over your workday. Physical and mental health are very important to every aspect of life. Physically, we know that when we are fit, well-rested, and healthy, we feel like we can conquer anything. When we overeat and when we are sleep-deprived, every situation seems to be doomed for failure. As an example, we know that when we eat a heavy meal for lunch, it is difficult to stay awake and concentrate for the rest of the afternoon. From a mental health perspective, we also know how difficult it is to concentrate and be productive when we are depressed or anxious, or when we are focusing on a personal problem from which we are suffering. We can't ignore the importance of our physical and mental health on our work life. If these areas need improvement, work with professionals as needed to get your physical and mental health on track. There are hundreds of reputable fitness trainers online who can help you get on a regular exercise program, as well as hundreds of licensed online therapists or life coaches to help you work through issues. We all have our issues. Seeking outside help can be a real game-changer.

Workplace or Organizational Health

Organizational health is also very important. Again, I am not an expert on this topic, but it does have an impact on one's performance. We know how difficult it is sometimes to focus in an environment that is negative or unhealthy. We know how difficult it is to operate in an environment full of drama and distrust. As such, we need to examine ways to improve workplace health. I am not a subject matter expert on this, but a great starting point that I recommend is *Five Dysfunctions of a Team* by Patrick Lencioni and *The Infinite Game* by Simon Sinek. Both have multiple books in publication. I would also highly recommend Simon Sinek's talks on organizational health and leadership. Search Simon on YouTube to watch a few of his videos. He is fantastic, and an inspiration.

Learn a Time, Task, and Email Management Methodology

We need an effective way to (1) process the hundreds of digital and human interruptions/tasks that we receive during the course of a day, and (2) organize the tasks, digital information, and paper information that hits our desk. In other words, we need a digital methodology to get organized—and stay organized. If we don't have system in place, we will operate in state of chaos. Studies show that if we do not have an effective task management system to capture our tasks and file away that information, we continue to worry about those things, which has an enormous impact on our ability to focus. I am an advocate of using and customizing tools like Microsoft Outlook and our smartphones to process this information. For those of you in the legal profession handling enormous volumes of documents, I also think that legal document management systems can be extremely helpful to legal professionals. These are tools like Worldox, NetDocuments, or iManage. For other professionals, tools like Microsoft SharePoint, customized for your organization's document management would be invaluable.

Attention Management Strategies

I want to share some essential attention management practices that are easy, practical, and will make an immediate impact on your ability to focus:

Turn Off ALL Digital Notifications.

We all should be aware of the perilous cost of task-switching. Notifications are invitations to task-switch. They are like a dozen little devils sitting on our shoulder, tempting us to do everything except what we are supposed to be doing, and those devils have a direct hotline to our brain. Why would we give the world a hotline to our brain? Turn all notifications off—and I mean ALL of them! In Outlook, email notifications can be turned off by navigating to **File > Options > Mail** and deselecting the four different methods of notifying you when a new message arrives.

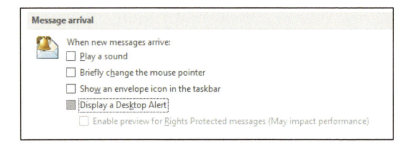

In Gmail, navigate to **Settings > Desktop Notifications** and turn mail notifications off.

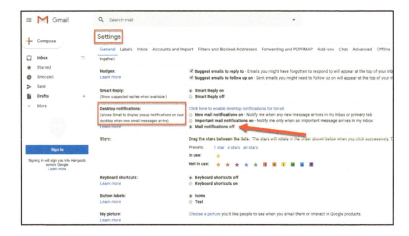

On an iPhone, go to **Settings > Notifications** and go through and turn off notifications by App. On an Android-based phone, go to **Settings > Notifications > Application Manager**, then turn off notifications by App.

Practice Single Tasking

It is not enough to say that multi-tasking is bad. We need to practice single tasking. We need to clear our desks AND our multiple monitors of information that is not directly relevant to the project that we are executing. For example, you should almost always minimize Outlook on your second monitor while you are working on projects unless you are using that information for the task that you are performing on your main monitor. Why would you leave up on your beautiful 21" screen the single most chaotic distraction known to man in the 21st century—email? That is insane if you think about it. Email fires distraction bombs at us every 30 seconds to 5 minutes. How can we possibly focus if we see those bombs land in our inbox? Just because we have 2 or 3 monitors doesn't mean that we need to have something displayed on them, especially if the information displayed on them derails our ability to focus on the task in front of us.

Pomodoro Technique ®

The Pomodoro Technique is a wonderful and easy technique that utilizes a 25-minute timer to maximize attention for a single task. Pomodoro involves single tasking for 25 minutes and then taking a break and doing something relaxing for 5 minutes. In other words, working in intervals. The human brain functions very well maintaining attention to a single task for 25 minutes. After 25 minutes, we begin to lose focus. By giving ourselves a 5-minute break, we can return to deep-thought work for another 25 minutes very easily.

After you get used to concentrating for 25 minutes, one can adjust the concentration interval to a longer time. Many people are able to work for 40 minutes or longer and take a 10-minute break. I often go 50-minutes now that I have expanded my initial non-existent attention span. The Pomodoro Technique makes a huge impact on productivity and also helps combat procrastination. Think about it, we can endure even the most tedious dreaded task for 25 minutes, right? Once we get a little momentum going and we get immersed in the project, it becomes a lot easier and you don't want to stop.

One important note: I recommend that you do not process emails during your break. Take a real break and do something relaxing, like getting some fresh air or water, or taking a 2-3 minute walk without your phone.

There are many other great time management techniques that are part of the Pomodoro way. To learn more, visit https://francescocirillo.com/pages/pomodoro-technique.

Tackle Deep-Thought Work Early in the Day (or when rested)

Dive into deep-thought work, like writing projects, early in the morning. There is little question about it—our brains function better following quiet time or sleep. We also know that we can be highly productive while the rest of the world is sleeping because there are far fewer interruptions. This can be one of the most productive times of the day.

Create Rituals

Rituals are short checklists designed to execute the same desired tasks during a set period of time—for example, a morning ritual. Rituals keep us on task. They are extremely helpful because they help us form positive habits and prevent us from getting distracted. As an example, I have a morning administrative ritual from 8 am to 10 am whenever I am in the office (when I am not traveling, speaking, or teaching). I avoid appointments with anyone during that time period unless it is urgent or extremely important. My morning ritual looks something like this:

- ✓ Review my Daily Plan that I created the day before (see below)
- ✓ Eat breakfast at my desk (oatmeal)
- ✓ Take my fish oil, garlic & vitamins
- ✓ 5-minute huddle with my team (as a group, or shorter with individuals)
- ✓ Reach out to one new organization for business development (speaking)
- ✓ Ask a potential client or existing client to grab coffee or virtual coffee via Zoom
- ✓ Review my potential new client report
- ✓ Reach out to past clients without active matters to check in

- ✓ Engage in business social media and send birthday wishes
- ✓ Check in with my leadership team members
- ✓ Check in with my partners

I don't get all these items finished each day, but I certainly do all of them at least twice a week. What I don't get completed today, I pick up where I left off tomorrow.

Rituals also remind us to do things that we frequently forget . . . things that we commit ourselves to do as New Year resolutions or annual goals. By adding rituals and checklists into your life, you can greatly enhance your ability to focus and do those things that seem to always fall off the radar.

Checklists can also be extremely helpful for enhancing our ability to focus. I discovered an awesome app for the iPhone/iPad called Simple Checklist to organize all my daily rituals and checklists. If you have an Android-based device, there is Chore Checklist or Habitica. One can use an app like this for other important checklists, like an Opening File Checklist, Closing File Checklist, Mergers & Acquisitions, Client Interviews, etc. I also use an app like this for personal things like "Winterize House Checklist" (turn off water spickets, clear garden, prep rose bushes, clean gutters, bring in ceramic pots, etc.) or "Monthly Home Tasks" (dog's heartworm, replace furnace filter, replace water filter, refrigerator filter, etc.).

Engage in Daily Planning

Daily planning is critical if you want to achieve focus and change your habits. If your current routine doesn't include daily planning, that routine must be broken and reconstructed. The reality is that very few people take the needed 5 to 10 minutes at beginning of the day or the end of the previous day that will save them hours, days, weeks, months, and years of waste and inefficiency. Most people just dive in or "show up." We jump right into email, where we become instantly derailed by fighting little fires instead of creating clear goals or a roadmap for the day. We need to sketch a daily plan, huddle with our team, adjust our daily plan if needed, and then use that daily plan as our roadmap to keep us focused. Without a roadmap, it is incredibly easy to allow distractions to control you. If you don't have a plan, you will quickly become part of someone else's plan.

Many people experience success by planning the next day's roadmap at the end of the day. We know where we left off with tasks and can plan where to begin again the following day. Others successfully engage in daily planning the morning before the day starts, when we are well rested and with a clear mind. If you engage in morning planning, I recommend coming in 10-15 minutes early to do so, before the day's fires have started. It is difficult to focus once the chaos begins, especially without a solid road map for the day.

Engage in Weekly Planning

A once-a-week "get organized" deep dive is essential to successful distraction and time management. This will help you frame realistic daily planning, catch things that "slip between the cracks," and keep you focused on the big picture goals that you want to achieve. It will help you stay driven and will give you the power of creativity and sense of control in your day and in your life. Do you want to move a mountain in your lifetime or just shift piles of dirt aimlessly? Without engaging in a weekly planning habit, you are just shifting around piles of dirt on the same mountainside.

As explained below in the chapter on weekly planning, I recommend this being a very disciplined practice that is rarely ever missed. Schedule everything around it as much as possible. Do it at the same time every week. For me, I do my weekly deep dive on Friday morning before the day starts.

In Chapter 2, there is a checklist of things to do during your weekly deep dive. Further, the chapter explains in detail how to execute each item in the checklist.

Digital Detox—A Balanced Approach

Many people view digital detox as "going off the grid." While I love the idea of doing that a couple times a year for a few days, it isn't very realistic for many professionals, and it certainly isn't very practical on a day-to-day basis.

A better way of thinking about digital detox is setting healthy boundaries. You want to set boundaries that still give you some freedom and joy, but also set you up for personal and professional success.

Here are some *examples* of healthy boundaries. Adjust the values/times to fit *your* needs.

Screen Scheduling

- No devices after 9 pm
- No email after 7 pm
- Phone-free food
- Phone-free walks
- Phone-free gardening
- I will spend no more than a total of 30 minutes per day on social media
- Social media-free Sundays

Volunteer Work

- I will serve on no more than 1 board at any one time
- I will serve on no more than 1 association committee at any one time
- I will limit non-billable administrative tasks to 10 hours a week
- I will handle 1 new pro bono case every other month

Personal Relationships

While boundaries are usually articulated in the negative (i.e., "I will *not* spend more than 30 minutes a day on social media"), relationship boundaries sound a little better stated the other way around.

- I will have 1 date night per week with my significant other
- I will go running or exercise with my children 2 times per week

Dietary, Exercise, and Health

- I will not eat between the hours of 7 pm and 10 am
- I will eat no more than 250 calories a day of junk food (e.g., chips or sugary food)
- I will limit my animal protein intake to 5% of my total diet
- I will drink no more than 2 caffeinated drinks per day
- I will drink no more than 1 alcoholic drink per day (and I will not accumulate them until the end of the week and drink them all at once).
- I will not get less than 7 hours of sleep every night.
- I will not consume less than 1 gallon of filtered water per day.
- I will not neglect my mental health. I will meditate once a day.

Chapter 2.

Email Management

The Email Problem

The typical professional today sends and receives between 100 and 200 messages daily. While we are discovering new ways to communicate via instant messaging and applications like Microsoft Teams, email is still one of the most important technological communication advancements of the past 100 years. It has fundamentally changed the way we communicate and do business.

For some professionals providing services like legal, accounting and consulting, emails present a wide array of issues that most of the business world will never face. In this chapter, we will discuss these issues and teach you how best to deal with them. These issues or problems range from ethical considerations to email overload and time-management. While there is no perfect solution, there are many methods to effectively handle large volumes of email.

The first step to solving any problem is understanding the problems that exist. We must get our arms around all the email issues that we face. The second step is to isolate each problem and tackle each one, without forgetting how that might impact other email problems. For instance, controlling spam email too militantly may prevent you from getting an important email from a client if your spam filter inadvertently catches an email from a client. In other words, when you solve one problem, it may open-up a different can or worms.

Methodology to Conquer Email—Your Game Plan

Most people do not have a methodology or a "plan" to process emails. Most people just blindly dive into email at the start of the day. However, developing a plan to process emails can vastly improve your workday efficiency. What follows is a logical game plan or methodology to process your emails. Adjust the items as needed.

Reduce the Number of Emails You Receive

We often focus on how to eat through all our emails, but we fail to think about ways to actually reduce email. Here are some practical ways to significantly reduce the amount of email that you receive.

1. Resolve email instead of kicking the can down the road. When we kick the can down the road, we often cause other problems and end up getting dozens more emails stemming from the original email.

2. Don't create 10 more emails from your response. As one example, when trying to schedule an appointment with someone or multiple people, use applications like Doodle or Microsoft FindTime. I like Microsoft FindTime because it is free with Microsoft 365 and it integrates directly with your calendar and contacts in Outlook. Too many people send an email like this: "How about setting up a meeting next week sometime?" If you sent that email to just 5 people, you are going to get 5-10 emails back with responses everywhere from "Sure" to "I have to take my pet to the vet" to "How about Tuesday at 4, or Wednesday at 3, 4 or 5, or Friday at 8, 9, 3, 3:30. . . ." In other words, it creates a total mess of emails that you have to piece together like a puzzle. It is like herding cats. Instead, send a quick, easy-to-create poll with FindTime or Doodle so that everyone can vote on their preferred times. These apps hold all proposed dates on your calendar as tentative until the poll is closed and you, as the organizer, pick the final time. Then it sends the invitation

out to all participants. It makes herding cats as easy as pie and eliminates blowing up everyone's inbox.

3. Be specific, not vague, in your emails, so you don't get 10 more questions. If people don't understand your answer, they are going to email you or others, causing even more email traffic and potential drama. Be clear in your responses. If it is too much to type, consider picking up the phone, or having a Zoom or Microsoft Teams call with video and screen-sharing to offer more clarity to your response.

4. Dial down the number of people that you and people in your office CC, BCC, or send group emails. Copy only the people who need to read the message.

5. Give your staff permission to not say thank you. Getting 30 emails that just say "thanks" will clutter your inbox, increasing the likelihood that an important email gets sandwiched and lost in between all the "thank you" emails.

6. Get a spam filter or fine-tune your existing spam filter.

7. Pick up the phone or get out of your chair and have an in-person conversation rather than sending an email. This will avoid a great deal of misunderstandings that cause drama and a dozen more emails. Have the in-person or phone

conversation, and then send the confirming email summarizing the solution.

8. Increase the use of Instant Messaging apps like Microsoft Teams or Slack.

9. Out of Office Notifications. Use them sparingly so people stop emailing you when you are out and avoid potential disasters. Don't overuse them. Don't rudely pepper other people's mailboxes with auto-responses. Finally, don't forget to turn them off when you return!

10. Use Outlook rules to auto-route emails from listservs and other similar senders into special inbox subfolders that you can visit when needed.

Process Emails Faster and More Efficiently with Templates or AutoText Entries

We all have email responses that are formulaic that we have to retype over and over again. Sometimes we spend several minutes looking for a similar email that we drafted recently to another person. Instead of wasting time retyping or looking for that similar email, we need to be able to process these emails more efficiently. We automate the creation of documents using forms, macros, precedents, or templates, so why wouldn't we automate the emails that we frequently draft? Instead of wasting time re-inventing the wheel or looking for older email responses, create an email template or an AutoText entry in Outlook to automate the response.

Email Templates

Email Templates are part of Microsoft 365. If you don't have a subscription to Microsoft 365, you will not have this feature available. Instead, use AutoText entries instead (instructions below).

1. Select **New Email** to create a new email.

2. Select **View Templates** from the Message ribbon. If you do not have this option, you need to download Microsoft 365 or update your version of Microsoft 365 for Outlook.

3. To create a new template, select the **+ Template** button located at the bottom of the My Templates pane.

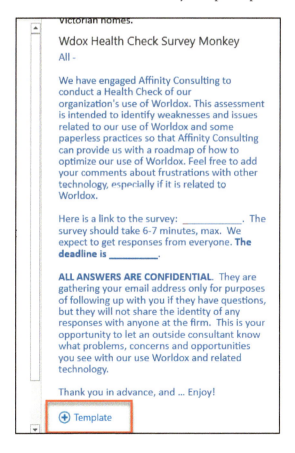

Name your Template, insert the desired text and hit **Save**.

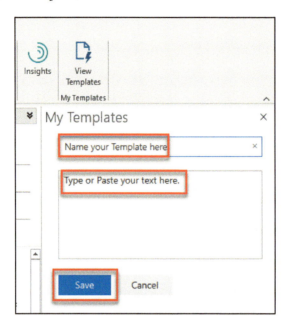

To insert the text from a template into an email, simply click on the desired entry and it will insert wherever your cursor is position in the email.

AutoText Entries

1. Find the "model text" that you want to use as the AutoText entry. Copy it into your Windows clipboard (select the text and hit **Ctrl + C**).

2. Draft a new email and paste it into the body of the new email (use **Ctrl + V** to paste). Format the text and clean it up. I suggest removing any client names, addresses, etc.— make it generic.

3. Select the text and then select **Insert > Quick Parts > AutoText > Save Selection to AutoText Gallery**.

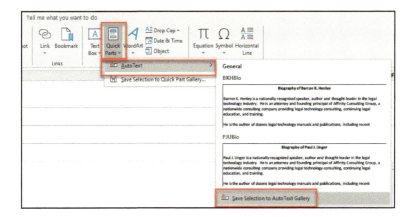

5. Give it a name (nickname) using at least 4 characters.

6. To insert the AutoText entry, simply place your cursor in the body of the email (in the desired location), and then type the first 4 characters of the AutoText name. You will see a pop-up preview of your entry. If you want to insert it, simply hit your **Enter** key. Another way to insert it is to select **Insert > Quick Parts > AutoText >** and then select the AutoText entry from the preview gallery.

If you like the idea of AutoText entries, but would like these handy text snippets to be available in other programs and on other devices, you should invest in a tool like TextExpander (www.textexpander.com), which costs less than $5 per month per user. Your text snippets are stored securely in the cloud and available across all your programs and devices. If you create or update one of your text snippets on one device, the update synchronizes across all your devices. It is also ecosystem agnostic, so it works on PCs, Macs, iDevices, and Android-based devices.

Allow a Trusted Assistant to Help Process Your Email

If you get more than 125 emails a day, think about allowing a trusted assistant to open your email help you process it and respond. I realize this may not be possible right away, and may never be possible for some people, but if it is, you should strongly consider it. First and foremost, you need an assistant that you can trust with sensitive information. Second, you may need to set up an alternative email account for you to receive HR-related emails or other sensitive emails. This would be an email account that your assistant would *not* see. Third, you need to contact your IT folks to have them set this up. Only your Microsoft Exchange administrator would be able to give these permissions to your assistant.

Batch Process Emails

Most professionals need to be more deliberate about when they check emails instead of checking email 70+ times a day or leaving their Outlook inbox maximized all day long. We need to reduce the number of interruptions (email and otherwise) so we can be more focused. After all, how on earth can anyone get anything done with an interruption every 2 to 3 minutes?

Ask yourself the following question: 10 or 20 years ago, would you have let someone walk in your office every 2 to 3 minutes offering to sell you a product or asking you for a favor? Of course, you wouldn't! So, why do you let it happen now with email? Why do you drop everything that you are doing to read and/or respond to an email that just arrived? You have invested thousands of dollars in technology that is supposed to make you more efficient, but instead it has created an interruption hotline to your brain.

Some time management experts suggest checking email twice a day. While this may sound like a good plan to some, it is completely unrealistic for most busy professionals. When email was just becoming popular, there wasn't an expectation that it would be dealt with immediately, so twice a day was probably okay. However, in today's age, checking email only twice a day is unrealistic and potentially irresponsible. Entire companies communicate via email. Email is a way of life and the way everyone communicates. Checking email twice a day isn't enough if you get 100+ emails—it would be overwhelming to sift through that many emails during two sessions. I think checking it throughout the day is more realistic, and just as important, will make it easier for you to prevent your inbox from getting out of control.

One way to handle this is to batch process emails at more planned or deliberate times. Some professionals simply cannot do this, since they live, breathe, and communicate via email instead of face-to-face or phone meetings. However, most professionals can engage in more batch processing at some level. Remember, we are talking about being more deliberate about when to check email instead of checking it 70+ times a day. If you can handle emails at more deliberate times, you could get more project work completed and follow your plan for the day.

Everyone's email batch processing schedule will be different, and it will probably change every day for most people. Some individuals must leave their email maximized on their screen all day or they will be fired! Others can get away with checking email just 2 to 3 times a day. I think most professionals fall somewhere in between those two extremes. It depends on your role and job description within the organization. Whatever the case, take a couple minutes at the beginning of the day to sketch a quick batch processing plan for your day. Here is an example:

Today's Batch Email Processing	
7:30 AM	15 minutes
10:00 AM	30 minutes
12 Noon	90 minutes
4:00 pm	30 minutes
5:00 pm	15 minutes

You will probably not stick to it 100%, but that is okay. Planning to check it 5 times and ending up checking it 7 or 8 times is still much better than checking it 70 times or leaving it maximized all day long on a second monitor. Also remember that every day will be different. Some days you will have no time to batch process emails. Other days, you may have the entire day.

Touch the Email One Time + 3-Minute Rule

Experts tell us it takes on average, 2-3 minutes to read and digest an email. Then we are forced to make a decision. What are you going to do with this email? Before you skip an email, or for that matter, any bit of information that comes across your desk (paper or digital), always stop and ask yourself, "What do I have to do to touch this just one time?" If you delay resolving it or acting on it, you are kicking the can down the road, and you are going to waste another 2-3 minutes the next time that you touch it. As such, always try to touch every email only once!

Delete, Do, Delegate, and Delay

When processing or attacking your email, and following the 3-minute rule, what should you do with the email after you initially review it? Here are your options: The 4 Ds. This is a slightly modified technique that I learned nearly two-decades ago from David Allen in his life-changing book *Getting Things Done®*. I have modified it to better fit the needs of professionals like attorneys, accountants, consultants, etc. who receive not just more email, but also more substantive and longer emails.

DELETE

DO

DELEGATE

DELAY

Remember, any email that can be responded to or dealt with within 3 minutes (saved in a client file, forwarded, deleted, etc.) should be dealt with immediately—the first time you lay eyes on it. This rule is based on the premise that the second time you have to deal with the email, it will again take you another 3 minutes to navigate to it, open it, read it, comprehend it, re-familiarize yourself with the topic and then handle it. So, why not just respond to it or delegate it immediately instead of wasting another 3 minutes at a later date? Stop procrastinating and re-wasting that 3 minutes over and over.

My 3-minute rule is a slight modification of David Allen's *Getting Things Done®* 2-minute rule in 2 important ways:

1. Most emails concerning matters in the legal community and many other professions take longer than 2 minutes, so I

increased response time to 3-minutes. If you sell widgets, 1 or 2 minutes may be all you need to process most emails.

2. It usually takes much longer than 2 minutes to read and respond to emails in the legal world. Often, lawyers and other professionals research and carefully craft a response from well-chosen words. It could take 30 minutes, 2 hours, or even days! The critical question to ask is if you have time to resolve the email in the time that you have allocated to batch process, then you should just resolve it. For example, let's say you have 1 hour allocated to batch process emails, and you encounter one email that will take 30 minutes to read and resolve. In that case, you should probably do it, especially if it is an urgent or a high priority. If it is going to take close to an hour or longer, then you may delay it. If you delay it, you are going to process the email by following the procedure below about how to properly delay and get the email out of your inbox. Remember the key to the 3-minute rule is that you avoid or minimize having to process an email more than once.

Delete

Delete whatever you can immediately. Learn how to use the DELETE key.

That should be the first thing that you do before you start dealing with email, just like *not* bringing junk mail and annoying advertisements into your home. It is easier to work from shorter lists than long list, so if you can get your list of unread emails from 20 down to 12, do it! Skim your inbox and **delete** the following:

- All the spam email that gets past your spam filter.

- Interoffice spam that is irrelevant to you.

- CCs that you don't need to save.

- Annoying jokes from friends and coworkers.

- Email from people you don't like (unless it's important, of course).

Tip—Delete Large Chunks of Email

Outlook Tip—Delete Large Chunks of Email

Sort email based on the **From** field (by clicking on the **From** column header). You can often get rid of large chunks of email sent from the same person. Select a chunk of email by single left-clicking on the first email, holding the shift key down and single left-clicking on the last email. Then hit **Delete**.

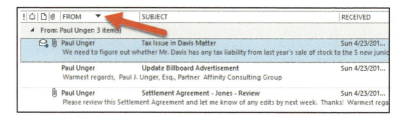

Tip—Clean up Conversation Threads

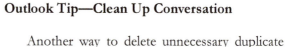

Outlook Tip—Clean Up Conversation

Another way to delete unnecessary duplicate emails from a conversation thread is to select one of the emails and then from the **Home** ribbon, select **Clean Up Conversation**.

Tame the Digital Chaos

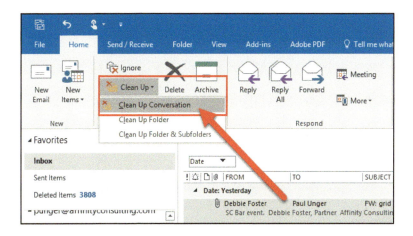

Tip—Delete Emails Permanently (Bypass Recycle Bin)

Outlook Tip—Delete Emails Permanently

By holding the **Shift** key down and hitting **Delete**, the email will be deleted from both your inbox *and* Deleted Items folder in one step. You will be asked to confirm if this is indeed what you want to do:

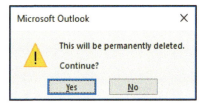

Do—Just Resolve it!

This is easy to explain, but hard to execute. If you can answer the question, make the decision, provide the solution, and bring it to a resolution, then just do it! Do not forget that you *may* be able to deal with it more quickly by picking up the phone or walking around the corner and talking with someone. Remember, an email oftentimes invites another email.

The problem with DO is that you must be organized in order to "do the do." In other words, if you are disorganized and can't find the answer to a question, then you will never be able to efficiently "do the do!" If you struggle with organizing digital information, I recommend my digital book *Fight the Paper* (2019), available at pauljunger.com.

Finally, if it is an email that is going to take a while, you have to exercise discretion about resolving it now or delaying. If you have time within your allotted batch process period, then go ahead and do it. If not, think about disposing of it in under 3 minutes by Delaying (below). Add it to your task list and calendar *then* move/save the email into the appropriate client/matter file.

Delegate

Much of the email that we receive today should be delegated to someone else, or we need an answer from someone else before we can respond.

If someone else should be handling the task or issue in the email, hand it off appropriately. Don't let someone else put "the monkey" back on you, in the words of *The One Minute Manager Meets the Monkey* by Kenneth Blanchard. You can make these emails and tasks easy to track by setting up a Follow-Up Items Outlook rule described below or use a Quickstep. Be sure that you have a system in place to follow-up on everything that you delegate so you can hold people accountable and the tasks you have delegated get done.

If you delegate or forward an email to someone, or ask for an answer from someone else so you can respond, do you have a system in place to track so you can follow-up on the issue without leaving the email in your inbox? Do people neglect to respond to you on delegated items? Do you sometimes find yourself trying to figure out when and to whom you delegated an item? If so, you may be responsible for enabling this behavior because you do not have a system in place to hold people accountable for tasks that you have delegated. Have you become that "push-over" that everyone ignores and your emails land in world of Neverland?

Here is a rock-solid technology solution that will help you with delegated items or follow-up items that originate from an email.

Follow-Up Items Rule

We delegate tasks to folks via email all day. We also ask people for information, but have a difficult time remembering to follow up on those items, resulting in things slipping between the cracks. One way to track those items is by creating an Outlook Rule to "capture" all those items that you are expecting others to do for you. Here is an Outlook Rule that will help.

This Rule looks for emails where you are the sender and where you copied yourself. It will automatically route those specific emails into a special folder called Follow-Up Items, so you have a dedicated folder with only delegated or follow-up tasks that you can review once a day. When I review those items, I usually forward those emails to people and politely ask them to update me on the status.

Here are the steps.

1. First, create a folder in Outlook called something like "!Follow-Up Items". Use an exclamation mark at the beginning of the name so it sorts alphabetically and displays at the top of your inbox subfolder list:

2. In Outlook, click on the **File** menu > **Manage Rules and Alerts** > **New Rule** button.

3. Choose **Apply rule on messages I receive** (that translates to "Apply this rule after the message arrives") and click **Next** at the bottom of the dialog.

4. Under **Select Conditions**, check BOTH **from people or public group** and **where my name is in the CC box**. At the bottom of the dialog, click the hyperlink for "people or public group" and add your email address. This basically creates a rule that will look for emails from you that are also copied to yourself. Click **Next**.

5. Under "Select Actions . . . What do you want to do with the message," choose **move it to the specified folder**. Select the folder that you created called "!Follow-Up Items." If you didn't create the folder yet, you can do it also at this stage. Click **Next** and add any exceptions (probably none). Click **Next**, and name it (something like "Follow-Up Items"), then click **Finish**.

Your final Rule should look something like this:

```
Rule description (click an underlined value to edit):
Apply this rule after the message arrives
where my name is in the Cc box
 and from Paul Unger
move it to the ! Delegated Items folder
```

Visit your Follow-up Items folder regularly. I recommend once a day. Open the items and determine if they have been resolved. If they have not been resolved, forward the email to the person who owes you the information or task and ask for the status: "Hi _____, what is the status of the attached? Please advise. Thanks!"

Delay—If Necessary

Oftentimes, we need delay a resolution until we have more time to research a topic or draft a longer mail. When we must delay, we should create a task, file the email in the appropriate matter or project folder, and then delete it from our inbox. If left in the inbox, it is likely to get buried by the avalanche of daily emails, and then forgotten until it is too late. We should not use our inbox as a task list.

Delayed emails generally fall into two categories: (1) a very temporary delay (meaning you can get to it in under a day); and (2) a delay of over a day or two. If the email requires only a very temporary delay, then just leave it in your inbox and process it later that day or the next morning. If the delay will be over a day or two, process it as follows.

As stated above in the 3-minute rule, if it is an email that is going to take a while to get to or complete, you should simply dispose of it in under 3-minutes by adding it to your task list and then saving it into the appropriate matter file. Stop using your Outlook inbox as a Task List! Instead, do the following:

1. Create a Task from the Email:

Drag and drop the email on to the task module in Outlook. This will convert the email to a task. This function acts as a copy and will leave the email in the inbox for you to take further action, like create a calendar deadline or file it away.

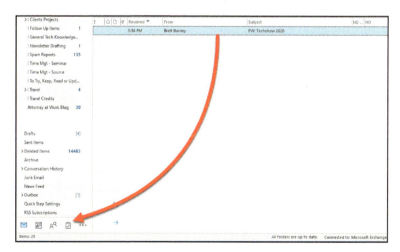

If you have multiple task lists/folders, I recommend that you open your email on one monitor and your tasks on the other monitor, and simply drag and drop emails into the desired task list.

Remember, this converts a copy of the email to a task, leaving the original email in your inbox to either file away or delete.

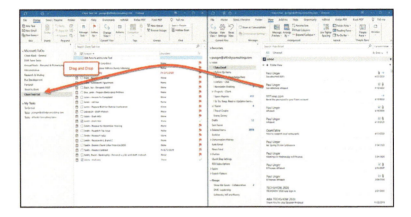

Alternatively, you can use **Quick Steps** to convert (copy) the email to a task item. To do this, select the email and then **Quick Steps > Create a Task**.

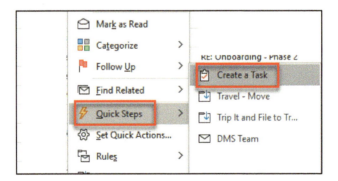

Other Guidelines on Delaying:

- If you still keep a paper-based task list (I hope not), simply write down the task associated with the email, and then save the email in the appropriate matter or project folder. If the appropriate place is still a paper file, print the email and place it in the paper file.

- In some circumstances, it is okay to set up subfolders under your inbox and place important emails there if you want to access them from your smartphone. For instance, if absolutely no one will ever need a copy of that email because you are a solo practitioner or business owner. Another example is when you want a copy of the email from your smartphone, and there is no other easy way to get it. If you save emails locally using this method, it is critical that you have a backup of your email data.

- If you only receive 10 to 20 emails a day, and you process your inbox down to zero (or close) every day, then it is probably okay to use your inbox as a task list. However, eventually, you will probably outgrow this, as your workload and email volume increases.

2. Record the Deadline on your Calendar:

After you have created a task, drag and drop the email onto the calendar module in Outlook. This will convert the email to an appointment. Again, this acts as a copy function and will leave the original email in the inbox for you to perform the next steps defined below.

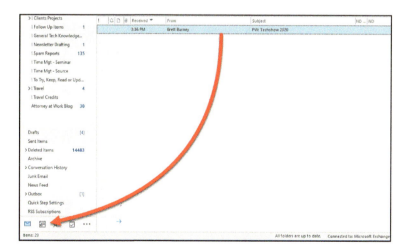

3. Schedule Time to Do It on your Calendar (Time Blocking):

Drag and drop the same email on the calendar one more time to create the appointment with yourself to do the work. If the response requires research and a block of time, schedule the time to do it. In other words, make an appointment with yourself. If you do not do this, you may find yourself up at 11 pm the night before it is due.

4. File/Move the Email from the Inbox:

File the email and delete it from your inbox. If your team needs access to the email, save it in a place where they can get to it. The correct place for this is within the digital matter or project folder located on your network in a Windows folder or in your electronic document management system. There are multiple ways of doing this, depending on the software that you have:

    a. **I only have Outlook.** If you only have Outlook, open the email, and select **File > Save As**. Save the email like you would save a Word document or PDF. For instance, save it into the correspondence folder and utilize the naming scheme YYYY-MM-DD - Long Name Description.

    b. **I only have Outlook, but I have dozens to move all at once.** In this case, open the desired folder through Windows Explorer on one monitor, and open your Outlook email list on another monitor. Next, select all the desired multiple emails and drag & drop them in bulk into the desired folder. Note that you may have to rename them because they will adopt the text in the Subject line as the file name. Alternatively, if you don't have a document management system or practice management system to extract these emails, there are some decent programs like SimplyFile / MessageSave by Tech Hit (www.techhit.com/messagesave) that can help you save emails out of your inbox and into shared folders on your network.

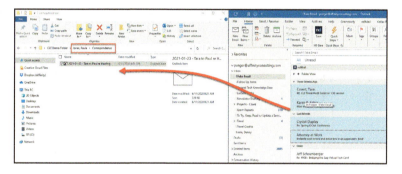

c. **I have a document management system like Worldox, NetDocuments or iManage, or a practice management system like Clio, Centerbase, PracticeMaster, etc.** If you have one of these systems, there are add-ins for Outlook that make it very easy to save emails. Below is a screen shot from NetDocuments (www.netdocuments.com), which demonstrates the simplicity of saving an email into a matter or project folder outside of your inbox. To save an email, simply select it and then select the desired matter from their prediction panel powered with AI/machine learning. This type of solution, by far, is the best and most ideal method for organizations that depend on heavy volumes of email. Many programs like these also offer "conversation thread filing" which can automatically save subsequent emails in the same thread to the matter.

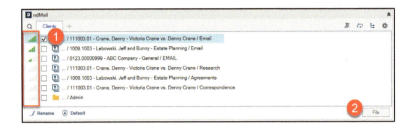

Summary

In summary, remember to try to process emails at more deliberate times, and touch the email only one time. What should you do with it? The 4 Ds—Delete, Do, Delegate, or Delay.

Remember the endgame. Ideally, you want to get the email out of your inbox so that (1) your inbox is "getting to zero"(or close to zero) on a daily basis; (2) any tasks and deadlines get recorded in your task list and calendar; (3) you have scheduled time to perform that task; and finally, (4) you are saving the email into the case/matter file where everyone on your team or in your office has access to it.

Treat Your Email Inbox Like Your U.S. Mailbox at Home—Clear it Daily!

Would you ever keep your U.S. Mailbox at home like your inbox in Outlook, with 1000+ items? Of course, you would not! So, do not let your digital inbox get that way.

For most people, maintaining email is the weakest link in their system of organization primarily because of volume and frequency. They use it as a holding bucket for undecided and unresolved tasks.

As stated above, the key to mastering your inbox is to process it to zero or as close to zero once a day. For most people, it is very helpful to be able to see all the emails in a single screen (or close to it). It is difficult and overwhelming to process emails and tasks when you are staring at a screen with 500+ emails.

Some email management strategies have suggested that getting to inbox zero is a waste of time. I disagree. If you are a salesman, teacher, landscaper, or you provide piano lessons (all noble professions), then maybe clearing your inbox is not a great use of your time. However, when you manage dozens (or 100+) legal matters, there is a much greater need, not to mention an ethical obligation, to manage case information properly. It is inappropriate to co-mingle documents from two separate matters. You greatly increase the risk violating your duty of confidentiality, not to mention the fact that your files would be a mess and it would take you exponentially longer to get anything done. In my opinion, that is unethical and a cybersecurity risk. Every professional that I speak with who follows the above methodology indicates that they are far more organized and focused than their counterparts who do not. Those who do not follow this methodology must hire more staff to read, process, and save the emails properly. In other words, if they don't do it, they hire someone who does.

Tip—Handling Paper Mail

Tip for Handling U.S. Mail at the Office and Home:

When picking up mail from your mailbox, receptionist, or mail room, recycle junk mail and advertisements before you get back to your desk or into your house. In other words, don't even let junk mail enter your workspace or your home. Stand over the recycling bin or shredder and immediately destroy all irrelevant mail. Don't give it the opportunity to pile up! Only bring mail into your workspace that is real/substantive. Also, to eliminate paper-based junk mail, consider the app PaperKarma (www.paperkarma.com). This app allows you to snap a photo of the junk mail, hit send, and it will automatically unsubscribe you from the mailing. It is available for iPhone and Android-based phones.

Chapter 3.

TASK AND DEADLINE MANAGEMENT

THE "TASK" PROBLEM

Task management is the process of capturing/recording tasks and executing them in an efficient manner.

Time management is how you utilize your time to execute the tasks on your plate. Although related to task management, time management is quite different.

Most of us struggle with both task and time management because we simply have too much to do in a given day. The reality is that urgency is a fact of life for a professional who provides critical services to individuals or businesses. As discussed above, we also constantly struggle with distractions and information overload. I have visited thousands of legal professionals over my career, and I have yet to encounter a law office or legal department that doesn't operate in that environment. Now, layer in technology, and most of us are even worse because we have let technology dazzle us to the point that we have lost most of our common sense. I am talking primarily about email, but it extends to social media, internet use, and apps on our mobile devices.

While technology can be blinding us to the solution, the beautiful thing about technology is that when it is paired with the right processes or methodology, it can efficiently solve quite a few problems. However, if you have bad processes in place, technology will fail.

BAD PROCESS VERSUS TECHNOLOGY? BAD PROCESS ALWAYS WINS.

Inefficient management of tasks and deadlines not only leads you to missing critical deadlines and having things "slip between the cracks," but also contributes greatly to your inability to focus, enjoy life, and sleep. Studies show that when we don't know what we have on our plate, we worry. Moreover, our subconscious goes into overdrive mode, which can cause anxiety, inability to focus, and inability to "be present." We must have a system in place to capture and organize tasks. If we don't, we are doomed to fail and be miserable.

One of the biggest problems with task management today is that many people still record all their tasks on paper, or they have them scattered and unorganized in some digital form (*i.e.*, stuck in their inbox). What I seek to do in the following chapters is to define a methodology for recording, organizing, and executing on tasks and deadlines, and then help you identify the right tool to use for organizing your tasks and deadlines.

THE PROCESS

Let's first cover the process, and then we will dive into selecting the right tool and how to use it. The process or methodology is versatile. It will work with any tool or software application. Understanding this will enable you to not only adapt whatever tool or software application that you use, but also "fix" what isn't working. Here are the 5 essential steps to the process:

1. Capture Tasks and Deadlines

2. Gathering and Getting Organized

3. Review and Revise – Weekly Deep Dive

4. Planning – Daily and Weekly Roadmap

5. Execution

Capture Tasks and Deadlines—Step One

Habitually capturing tasks and deadlines is critical to success. Currently, most people have tasks and deadlines scattered all over the place. Some in their calendar, some in a paper-based list, some in the case/matter/project file, some in their head, some within inboxes, and some who knows where else. I learned many years ago from David Allen's *Getting Things Done®* that it is critical that everyone has a "trusted bucket . . . that doesn't leak." In other words, we need a task-capturing system that truly captures everything that we must do and does not let things leak out. It must capture everything to be effective.

There are many reasons for capturing truly everything. First, we obviously do not want to miss any deadlines, commit malpractice, or disappoint anyone. We know how stressful that can be. Many people lose their jobs because they are disorganized, and they drop too many balls. Second, and equally important, studies now demonstrate that when we do not have everything written down or captured on a list, it can significantly impair our ability to focus.[1] In a time years ago with less infomania and information overload, we may have been able to rely more on our memories. However, in today's fast-paced world of social media, email, the 24-hour news cycle, etc., we just can't rely on our memories to do that heavy lifting! Failing to have things written down with a reasonable level of detail actually causes us anxiety. However, when we have everything recorded, and especially when we are organized, we experience a sense of control, and focus. In other words, when we know what is on our plate, it helps us focus and unleashes our creative powers.

Random Neural Firings—Record Everything

Get in the habit of immediately capturing and converting "random neural firings" to a written or recorded task. For instance, if while you are working on one project and you get a random neural firing about something that you need to do on another project, journal or record the other task right away. If you don't record it

---

1. E.J. Masicampo & R.F. Baumeister, *Consider It Done! Plan Making Can Eliminate the Cognitive Effects of Unfulfilled Goals*, JOURNAL OF PERSONALITY & SOCIAL PSYCHOLOGY (June 2011).

within 30 seconds, there is a 50/50 chance that you will forget about it. I think it is critical to have your task list immediately available to you so you can easily capture that task on your list. If it takes you too long to open and create a task, or if it is a cumbersome process, you probably won't do it. It must be easy and fast so you can get back to the original task at hand.

In summary, what you are looking for is a system that makes it easy for you to capture and organize all tasks. The more scattered and unorganized the system, the more likely that it will fail, so it is vital that you keep it simple. Below, we will specifically discuss different tools (paper, software, etc.).

Gathering and Getting Organized—Step Two

It is critical that you create a master task list that captures everything. You must dedicate time to gather all the tasks, piles, sticky notes, task lists, etc. and record those tasks into your system/tool of choice. I call this "Gathering and Getting Organized." Depending on how disorganized you are right now, the first time you do this could take a few hours, or more. However, this is an essential exercise and one of the first steps you must take. The process is gratifying. I equate it to when I first cleared the paper files off my desk nearly 20 years ago with my Xerox Documate 262 desktop scanner (pre-Fujitsu ScanSnap, which is now my desktop scanner of choice).

These items that you gather will be added to your "trusted bucket that doesn't leak," or your "Master Task List." At the end of the process, you will have a very clean desk, a long, but organized, central master task list, *and* all your piles and sticky notes will be gone. It is liberating!

> *"It's like that sigh & feeling of satisfaction when you clean out your garage or basement, . . . except with no back pain."*

Task Lists/Categories/Folders

Many time management experts develop elaborate and too many separate task lists. In my belief, these techniques tend to fail because they are too complicated and there are too many lists in too many places. For task management to work, it must be simple and convenient. It cannot take you six months to learn and master the system. Maintain just as many lists as you need, but not too many. As a starting point, think about using the following four categories for lists:

1. Client/General

2. Administrative

3. Business Development

4. Home/Personal

As you create tasks and get organized, you will enter them in one of these four lists. Most software tools allow you to see all the tasks combined in one giant list as well as separated into their own lists. For instance, in Outlook, the ToDo list is the one giant list that combines all the tasks that you have in your separate task lists. You may want or need to create other categories/lists. For instance, I have two more that I maintain that are extremely helpful to me:

1. Travel to Book

2. Research, Reading, and Writing

Remember the key is to have as many task lists as you need, but not too many. Err on the side of creating fewer and broader lists and adjust as needed.

Naming Tasks—Use Good Descriptions

It is critical that you use good descriptions when you name a task. This is important so the tasks are well-organized, but also because one of the primary reasons people procrastinate is that they don't know what they need to do next, or what the next step is. It may have been fresh on your mind when you created the task yesterday, but 50 other things have happened since then and now you have forgotten.

For example, "Work on Smithville Project" is probably a bad description.

Instead, be more specific in your descriptions *and* use a prefix in your naming scheme. For instance, as seen below, add "Smithville Project - " at the beginning of the description. This allows you to sort/group your tasks by client/matter/project because the list can be sorted alphabetically. Additionally, if you have a practice management program, having the client/matter name in the description will help you organize tasks that you need to associate to matters within those systems. Secondly, after the hyphen, use a good clear description like "Review Jones report for security issues and draft recommendations by October 15th." This tells you exactly what needs to be done next. You can also use the notes section to add additional details if you run out of space. In Chapter 4, below, we will discuss in more detail how tools like Microsoft ToDo allow you to create sub-tasks and other details for tasks. We will also cover more advanced functions.

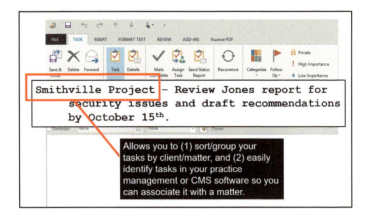

Step-by-Step Checklist for "Gathering and Getting Organized"

The good news for this step is you should only have to do this once. If you fall off the wagon and neglect your Weekly Deep Dives for a long period of time, don't fret. Since you already have the methodology and infrastructure in place, it won't take long to repeat the full process again. Here are the directions.

1. **Your Desk**

Start with cleaning up your desk and converting piles to tasks. Since your desk is your battle station, and you spend most of your time there, I think it is the most important place to clean up and therefore should be cleaned first.

   a. **Sticky Notes**. Collect all sticky notes, one at a time, and convert them to Tasks. Take this one as an example. This sticky note belongs as a task on the task list and perhaps as a deadline on the calendar (or docketed in your organization's docketing system if you have such a system).

Create a New Task in Microsoft ToDo (or similar tool)

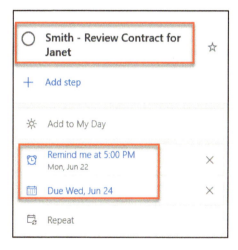

Next, add the deadline to your calendar.

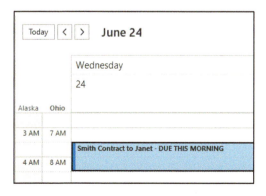

Then, block out or schedule time to work on the task a few days before it is due.

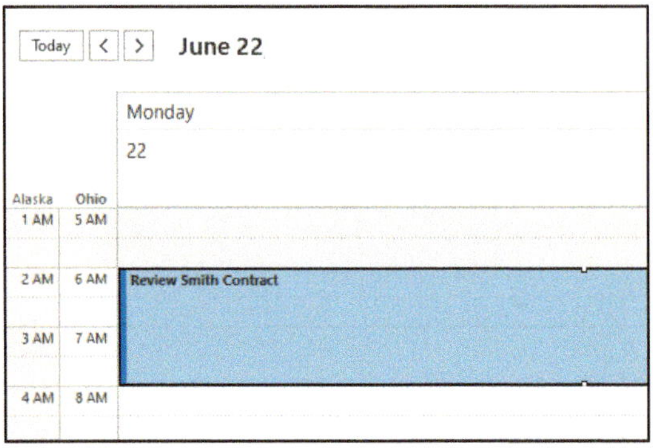

[Calendar screenshot showing June 22, Monday, with "Review Smith Contract" blocked from 6 AM to 8 AM]

Finally, throw the sticky note away, and move on to the next sticky note.

    b. **Lists on Legal Pads and Pieces of Paper.** Collect all lists from legal pads and other pieces of paper. Create a new task within your task list and create a deadline on your calendar for each item from all your lists.

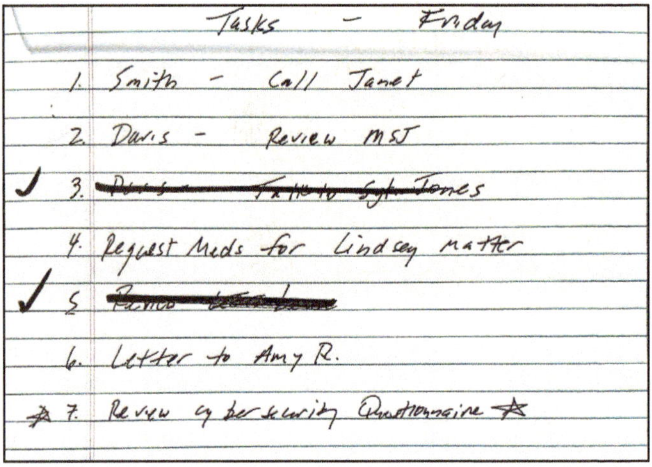

[Handwritten list: Tasks — Friday
1. Smith — Call Janet
2. Davis — Review MSJ
✓ 3. ~~Points~~ ~~Reply to Syd Jones~~
4. Request Meds for Lindsey matter
✓ 5. ~~Review~~
6. Letter to Amy R.
★ 7. Review of her security Questionnaire ★]

    c. **Paper Piles.** After you convert sticky notes to tasks and lists, do the exact same thing for documents, paper piles, etc. For instance, many people have rows of documents on their desk and treat the items within those rows as "tasks." In other words, their desk IS their task list. Sound familiar?

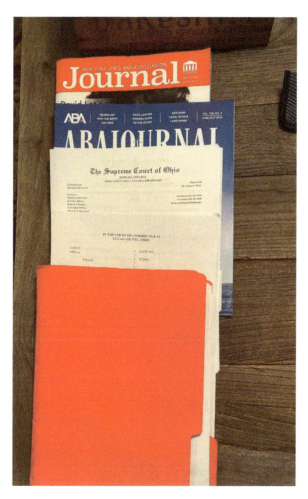

Each of the items pictured above is a task and probably has a deadline. Take each one and (1) create a task on your task list, (2) record the deadline on your calendar or docketing system, (3) schedule the time to do the task, if needed (time blocking), and then (4) scan the document and/or file it in the appropriate digital case/matter/project. I would then shred the document (not retaining the paper or keeping a paper file). If you aren't ready for that, then file the paper away in the appropriate physical storage location.

d. **Other "Things."** We also may have other things on our desk that are "tasks". For instance, right now, I have an antique metal Fritos lunch box on my desk because I want to sell it on eBay. I am using my desk as a reminder to sell it. Again, I am using my desk as a task list.

Put the item on your task list (*i.e.*, "Personal – list antique Fritos lunchbox on eBay"), and then put the lunchbox back on your shelf or in the basement. When you finally sell it, you can go grab it and mail it off to the buyer. Do not let it clutter your desk or brain.

On the flip side, there are times when putting an object like this on your desk is okay. Use your discretion. If you want to list the lunch box today and that is a good way to remind yourself to get it done today, then just do it. If you need to review the Smith contract today (perhaps it is due today), and you decide to put a paper copy next to your keyboard to help give yourself a big visual reminder— a kick in the butt to do it—and that works for you, then do it! However, if those items end up staying on your desk for days, and they pile up, that is when you are using your desk as a to do list and it becomes problematic. Exercise common sense and discretion.

e. **Someday Lists/Bucket Lists.** Many people maintain "someday" lists. Perhaps this is a list that you keep in a drawer. These are items like "Go skydiving," "Write a book," "Take Billy to Washington D.C.," or "Take parents to Italy." These items often times get lost and you don't find them until a life event occurs that makes it nearly impossible to complete the task. Don't make that mistake. Your someday or bucket list items should be part of your Master Task List. You should be reviewing those items at least monthly so you can make plans to do them and they do not get forgotten.

    f. **Personal Lists/Home Lists.** Unless it is inappropriate for you to do so, I usually encourage people to grab that personal list of things like home repairs, home tasks, etc., and combine that into your Master Task List. In most systems, you can separate these lists so they are not mixed in with your client tasks. Find this list and add these items to your new task list system.

    g. **Administrative Lists.** We all have administrative tasks such as marketing, rainmaking, committees, task forces, management. I typically advise people to add these items and lists into your Master Task List as well. Again, these can be on a separate list within your system, so they are not mixed with client tasks.

2. Your Credenza

Locate sticky notes, lists, documents and convert those, like described above, to tasks and then throw away the sticky note (or scan & save the document, and then throw away the physical paper).

3. Your Floor

Locate sticky notes, lists, and documents and convert those to tasks as described above, then throw away the sticky note (or scan and save the document, and then throw away the physical paper).

4. Your Briefcase, Purse, Computer Case

Locate sticky notes, lists, and documents in these locations and convert to tasks as described above, then throw away the sticky note (or scan and save the document, and then throw away the physical paper).

5. **Any In-Trays/Out-Trays**

Many people still have physical trays to collect incoming and outgoing paper-based mail, correspondence, memos, etc. Again, go through all these documents and be sure that you take each one and (1) create a task on your task list, (2) record the deadline on your calendar or docketing system, (3) schedule the time to do the task, if needed, and then (4) scan the document and file it in the appropriate digital case/matter/project.

6. **Other Places (Kitchen Counter, Car, Refrigerator Door, etc.)**

Basically, any other place where you accumulate tasks, sticky notes, piles, and lists—go through the same process of creating a task and blocking off time, then eliminate the paper copy of the reminder.

Review and Revision – Weekly Deep Dive—Step Three

Once a week, do a "Weekly Deep Dive" to update, and do a mini getting organized and gathering session. Because life happens, sometimes we jot something down quickly on a sticky note as we run out the door. Simply take one-hour each week to get organized and get rid of any piles, lists, or sticky notes. Clean up and update your Master Task List. I call this the "Weekly Deep Dive" and it is covered in depth, below.

Planning Your Daily & Weekly Roadmap—Step Four

Effective planning is a 5-minute commitment every day, and a 1-hour "Weekly Deep Dive" once a week. This is truly one of the easiest habits that you will ever form and has the biggest payoff of anything that you do. These two processes (Daily Planning and Weekly Deep Dive) are covered in depth below.

Execution—Step Five

It is one thing to have a comprehensive task list, be well-organized, and to have a great plan. It is another to execute on your tasks and complete tasks. Assuming that you have the motivation, creativity, knowledge, and skill to actually do the work (which I cannot help you with), there are five things that I *can* help you with that can set you up for successfully executing tasks: (1) setting aside time to do the work, (2) cultivating the mental clarity/focus to do it, (3) minimizing interruptions, (4) having reference material well organized and available, and (5) utilizing proper tools/software. We addressed 1 through 3, above, in earlier chapters. Reference materials/information and proper tools are covered below.

Things Never Go as Planned

Keep in mind that most professionals providing services to clients live in a "hair on fire" world. Our client's problems often become our fires. One cardinal rule of time management is that things never go as planned. Time management is about the constant renegotiation of deadlines. Don't let that discourage you. The key is that you have a methodology in place to process information and tasks so you can easily pivot to change your plan and still capture incoming tasks.

Rinse and Repeat

As one plan to execute a task gets derailed, and as one day ends and another day begins, it is important that we regroup, hit the reset button, and then restart. When your plan for today goes off the rails, take a moment to smile and be thankful for the business. Shake it off and regroup. Rinse and repeat.

Summary

In summary, this is the high-level process and the foundation. You can customize nearly any task management tool around this methodology.

1. Capture Tasks and Deadlines—you need to easily be able to capture tasks and deadlines.

2. Gather and Get Organized—you need to gather all your tasks into a master task list and get organized.

3. Review and Revision—you need to become intimately familiar with your tasks and update them.

4. Planning—you need to plan daily for 5 minutes and plan weekly for 1 hour.

5. Execution—you need to carve out time and follow time management principles to focus.

Chapter 4.

TASKS—THE RIGHT TOOL TO MANAGE TASKS

PAPER OR SOFTWARE?

It is critical that you have a tool to track tasks. To *not* have a tool is the biggest mistake. The human brain is incapable of memorizing so many tasks in today's age of information overload. It is best to use our brain on more important things like reading, writing, and analysis than to memorize hundreds of tasks and their deadlines.

I would rather someone have a paper task list than no task list at all. That said, I prefer the use of software for at least the Master Task List. Remember—keep things simple. I recommend the following:

1. A software-based task list for your Master Task List (*i.e.*, Microsoft ToDo, Outook, Gmail Tasks, Clio Tasks, etc.). Your Master Task List will likely store hundreds of tasks/items;

2. Paper for your daily road map/daily list of tasks. This list will have only 3 to 5 things and is kept next to your keyboard. Alternatively, a daily task list could be within a software application, like Microsoft ToDo's "My Day." We will discuss this below in Chapter 5 when one might be better than the other for you.

Why Digital Task Lists Failed You in the Past

Many people have tried using Outlook tasks in the past and failed miserably. There are two primary reasons for this. First, the interface for Outlook tasks is horrible. It is still horrible, to be honest. It looks like a cockpit of a 747. It just doesn't resonate with people. In large part, Outlook tasks have looked as ugly as they do now since Outlook became widely available in the early 1990s! Second, if you were out of the office and needed to create a task, it was impossible to create the task without going back to the office. As a result, tasks would instead get written down on sticky notes and napkins. Today, that problem is solved because we can now enter tasks directly on our smartphones, or simply tell Siri, Alexa, or Google (our virtual assistants) to create the task.

If Outlook or another digital task list failed you in the past, you need to give it another try because technology has improved immensely.

Why Software is Better than Paper for Your Master Task List

Keep in mind, that I do advocate the use of paper for **daily planning** (see below). That is primarily because (1) we need our computer monitors to display other important information, and (2) daily planning is extremely focused and contains a very short list of tasks (usually 3 to 5 items). We are always more focused on a daily basis when we operate from shorter lists. However, since the Master Task List usually contains 100+ items, software is definitely a better tool for the master task list.

Why software is better than paper for the master task list:

1. **One Centralized List.** With software, you have one centralized list, probably stored in the cloud and accessible from multiple devices.

2. **No Re-Writing.** With paper, you constantly have to re-write your lists. When you have 100+ items, that is a waste of time and opens the door for human error.

3. **Shareability and Collaboration.** Tasks maintained within software are sharable with internal and external users. One can have a project and assign tasks to multiple people. Best of all, you can track when those tasks are completed.

4. **Automatic digital reminders/notifications.** Software reminds you when tasks are due and will alert you ahead of time so you can plan to get them completed.

5. **Subtasks.** With software, you have the ability to create subtasks under a main task and track progress.

6. **Backup in Multiple Locations.** Software-based task lists provide data backup up in multiple locations, making tasks extremely difficult to lose, unlike a piece of paper.

7. **Capture and View from Any Device.** With software, you can enter tasks and view them from all your devices (computer, tablet, smartphone).

8. **Sortable Lists.** Software gives you the ability to sort your task list based on the due date, or the description, or the priority, etc. You can't sort anything on paper.

9. **Filterable Lists.** With a click of a button, software gives you the ability to display just the tasks assigned to me, or just the tasks due this week, etc. You can't filter anything on paper.

10. **Syncronization/Integration with other Programs.** Software typically provides the ability to synchronize between Outlook/smartphone/practice management software or contact management software, so all lists are synchronized and up-to-date in all programs and devices.

OUTLOOK TASKS AND MICROSOFT TODO

The process of task management must be convenient and simple. Outlook isn't perfect. In fact, it is kind of ugly, but it works well with my rules because of its convenience, ease, versatility, and ability to integrate with smartphones. If you cannot easily capture and record a random neural firing, thought, or task quickly and in a central location, that task will either be lost or quickly forgotten.

Outlook, along with your smartphone, is a viable solution. Before smartphones, maintaining a task list in Outlook was nearly impossible because you cannot carry your desktop computer around and you cannot wait 5 minutes for a laptop to boot up and start Outlook in order for you to record the task. Smartphones and tablets are instantly available. You can use Siri on an iPhone or iPad or voice commands on an Android device to create the reminder or task. There is no boot-up process. In fact, often times, it is faster than writing it on a random piece of paper. It is certainly better to record it on the smartphone because it can be instantly organized and, even more importantly, instantly backed up, thus far less likely to be lost like a piece of paper, sticky note, or a napkin.

Microsoft ToDo is a relatively new application that Microsoft developed after purchasing a wildly popular task list called Wunderlist. Microsoft finally sunset Wunderlist in 2020, forcing everyone into Microsoft ToDo. Based on everything that I have seen, Microsoft seems to have big plans for ToDo. In fact, if you log into Microsoft 365 today within your browser and open Tasks in Outlook, it is actually the Microsoft ToDo interface—not Outlook. That is great news.

The beauty behind all this is that Outlook synchronizes seamlessly with Microsoft ToDo. If you create a task in one, it shows up in the other instantly as long as you have Microsoft 365 with hosted Exchange (as most organizations do these days). If you don't have Microsoft 365 with hosted Exchange, I would recommend that you simply use Microsoft ToDo without Outlook, or Outlook (or another reliable tool) by itself.

Task Folders

I strongly recommend creating a small handful of necessary task folders (lists) to organize your tasks. Recall, we always focus and operate better from short lists. As indicated above regarding the process, I generally recommend four core task lists if you are an attorney in a law firm, an accountant serving clients from the general public, or someone in a similar profession. Create these four task folders (lists) in whatever system you are using:

1. Client—General

2. Administrative

3. Business Development

4. Home/Personal

For an attorney in a legal corporate department or college/university, or similar profession providing professional services, I usually recommend the following if you don't have to worry about business development:

1. General Legal Work

2. Administrative

3. Research and Writing

4. Home/Personal (although, you may want to manage a personal list in a separate personal system because of FOIA requests or computer corporate acceptable use policies)

To create a new Task Folder in Outlook, right click on **Tasks** and select **New Folder**.

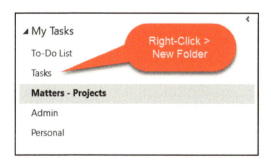

To create a new Task Folder in Microsoft ToDo, click on **+ New List** in the bottom-left corner, type in the desired description and hit **Enter**.

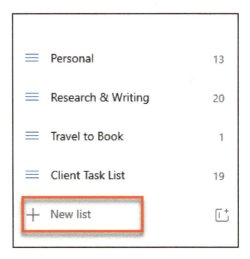

This is a screen shot of the Outlook Task List:

	!	@	Subject ▲	Due Date
			ABC Corp - Draft Corp Docs	None
			ABC Corp - Interview Witness Bunny Lebowski	None
			Davis - Research tax issue	None
			Davis - Settlement Agreement	None
			Davis, Joe - Research XY&Z	None
			Doe, John - Prepare Bankruptcy Petition	None
			Jones - Answer to Complaint	None
			Jones - call Joe	None
			Jones - Prepare Brief for Pretrial Conference	None
			Lebowski - Draft Motion	None
			Smith - Draft MSJ	None
			Smith - Prepare for November Hearing	None
			Smith - Research Tax Issue	None
			Smith - Research xy&z	None
			Smith - Reseearch A, B and C.	None
			Smith - Review Client Letter from 6/4/2020	None
			Smith - Review Contract for Janet	Wed 6/24/2020
			Smith, David - Bankruptcy - Research x y &z and draft contract.	None

This is the task list in Microsoft ToDo. As one can see, it is easier to read:

This is the identical task list in Microsoft ToDo when viewed from a smartphone:

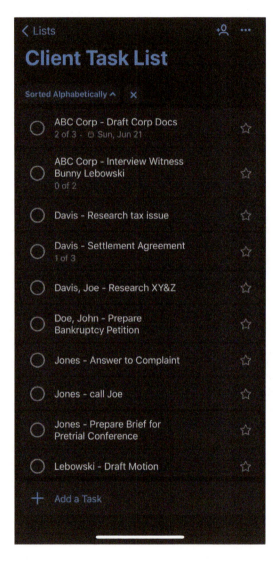

My recommendation to most people providing professional client services is to use Microsoft ToDo as the main task management tool, unless your organization has invested in a more specific software application. You should continue to use Outlook if you like to convert emails into Tasks. Recall they synchronize, so if you create a task in Outlook, it shows up immediately in ToDo. Also remember that a key part of email management is to stop using your inbox as a task list. Many emails remain in inboxes for the simple reason that they are really tasks. You must be able to convert them to tasks easily.

Recall also from Chapter 2, above, that within Outlook you can easily convert emails to tasks by simply dragging an email on to the task button. This is an important function.

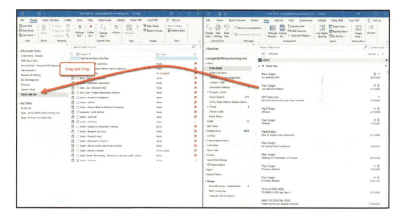

Additionally, if the email has attachments, you can right click then drag and drop on to the task button or task folder. When you right click, drag and drop, the attachments are embedded within the task, making it very convenient to start working on a particular document, or having all the reference material that you need at your fingertips in order to execute the task.

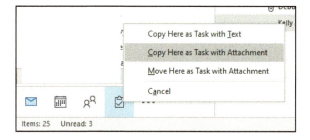

Once Microsoft creates an add-in to convert Outlook emails to a Microsoft ToDo task list item (which Wunderlist could do back in the day when it was widely used and available), then there will be no need to continue to use the older Outlook Task interface. As indicated previously, Microsoft knows how ugly and underutilized the Outlook task module is and will likely replace it completely with Microsoft ToDo. Hopefully, they will do this sooner rather than later.

Creating a Task in Outlook

Click on the desired task list, and then, to create a task within that list, click the **New Task** button in the upper left-hand corner, or drag and drop an email on to the task button or a specific task folder.

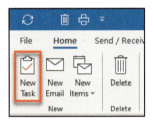

A New Task form will appear:

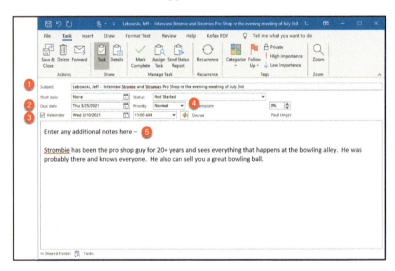

1. Enter the Subject starting with the name of the client/matter, followed by a description of the action item. By using the matter name at the beginning, you can group

all tasks for that matter together when you sort the subject alphabetically, as seen here:

- [ ] Jones - Prepare Brief for Pretrial Conference
- [ ] Lebowski, Jeff - Draft Motion to Extend Witness Disclosure
- [ ] Lebowski, Jeff - Interview Stombie the ProShop Dude
- [ ] Smith - Draft MSJ
- [ ] Smith - Prepare for November Hearing
- [ ] Smith - Research Tax Issue
- [ ] Smith - Research xy&z

2. (Optional) Enter a **Due Date** so that you can optionally view tasks with due dates and view those tasks in different colors.

3. (Optional) Add a **Reminder** if you so desire. I find these to be helpful for higher priority items.

4. (Optional) Set a **Priority** (High, Normal, Low). Not everything is a high priority, despite your feeling of being overwhelmed. Should you believe everything is urgent, then pretend you are categorizing the level of urgency. As a result, your day will consist of the following:

a. High = Urgent

b. Normal = Less Urgent

c. Low = Even Less Urgent

d. Someday Items = These are items that are more akin to New Year's resolutions, goals, or bucket list items. Add "Someday" to the beginning of the Subject line so they can be grouped together when sorted:

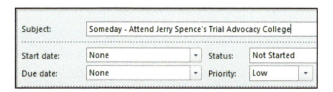

5. Enter any **Notes** in this area that you may find helpful or if you do not have enough room for a detailed description in the subject line.

e. Use the Notes section in Outlook to add subtasks or steps to complete the task. Unfortunately, these are not separate trackable tasks, so most people turn on the bullet or numbered list and start typing the subtasks. When complete, you can use the strikethrough font to indicate they have been completed. Microsoft ToDo actually has real subtasks, yet another reason to use ToDo rather than Outlook.

Creating a Task in Microsoft ToDo

Click on the desired task list, and then start typing in the **+ Add a task** field located at the bottom of that list.

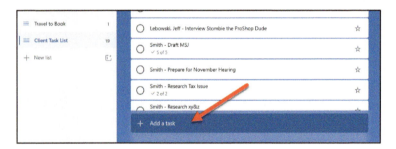

Complete the information needed to create the task:

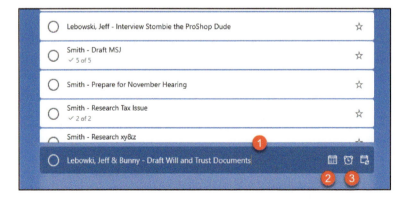

1. Enter description of the task. Just like with Outlook (or any digital task list), use the same naming scheme described above:
   Client/Matter Name - hyphen - good description of next step.

2. Add a Due Date, if desired.

3. Add a Reminder, if desired.

There are many other excellent features of Microsoft ToDo that are incredibly easy and intuitive.

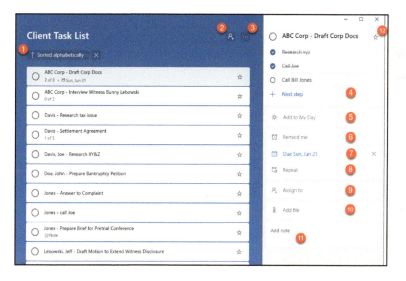

1. Sorting order for your list (by importance, due date, my day, alphabetically, creation date).

2. Share your list with internal or external users.

3. Print, email list, pin to start, delete list, or change sort order.

4. Set up steps or subtasks.

5. Add task to My Day, which is a way to create a daily task list from items already in your Master Task List.

6. Add or change reminder, if desired.

7. Add or change due date, if desired.

8. Designate if the task is a repeating task.

9. Assign the task to another person and still track it on your list.

10. Add documents/attachments.

11. Add any desired notes.

12. Tag a task as Important.

To access your lists and filtered lists, select the desired option along the left-hand side:

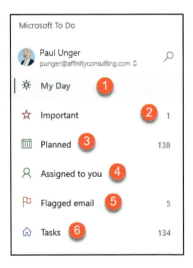

1. **My Day** is your daily task list if you want to use ToDo to create a daily task list.

2. **Important** is a filtered list that just shows tasks that you tagged as important (the star tag).

3. **Planned** will display those items with due dates.

4. **Assigned to You** will display any tasks that have been assigned to you.

5. **Flagged email** displays any email you have flagged.

6. **Tasks** show all tasks from all task lists in a combined listing.

Microsoft ToDo—Everywhere

Note: In order for your task lists to synchronize across devices and with Outlook, you need Microsoft 365 with hosted exchange. If your exchange is local, Outlook and ToDo will not synchronize. Check with your IT department to see if you have a hosted or local exchange server at your organization.

- **Desktop on your PC.** Download the ToDo application for Windows from your Office 365/Microsoft 365 login or the Microsoft online store (www.todo.microsoft.com). You will be prompted to login using your organization's Microsoft 365 credentials.

- **Desktop on your Mac.** Download the ToDo application for your Mac from your organization's Microsoft 365 login or the Microsoft online store (www.todo.microsoft.com). You will be prompted to login using your organization's Microsoft 365 credentials.

- **iPhone or Android-based Phone or Tablet.** You definitely will want to load the app on your smartphone (iPhone or Android based), as well as your tablet. The award-winning app for mobile devices has nearly all the functions of the desktop version. Download and install from the Apple store on your iPhone or Google Play App Store on your Android device. Again, you will be prompted to login using your organization's Microsoft 365 credentials.

- **Microsoft Online.** You can also access ToDo online (www.office.com/apps) from a browser.

Other Available Programs and Apps

There are a number of other outstanding options for tracking tasks. As I indicated earlier, the only mistake is not having a system at all. Here are some of the other options that you should consider. With all these options, keep a few things in mind:

- **Keep it Simple!** The more programs, the more complex, the more likely that things will fall apart.

- **Start with Fewer Lists.** It is easier to check 5 lists located in the same place than 5 lists in 3 different programs.

- **Get your Team on Board!** You are much more likely to use a task list if others on your team are using the same tool. You can also help each other with technical support and tips.

Other Task Lists

There are probably a hundred programs and/or apps available on the market. Task management is extremely personal. The way something looks and how you connect with it can make a big impact on its adoption and success. I kept this in mind as I reviewed applications and noticed a few features that stand out.

- The interface must be easy to use and resonate with users, ensuring your entire team will want to use it.

- The tool must make it simple to create and organize tasks.

- Synchronization between every platform you use is a necessity.

- It must offer multiple ways to organize your tasks based on lists, due dates, and sorting capability.

- The ability to share lists and tasks is essential.

If you are a law firm or legal department, also keep in mind the countless number of software tools on the market like NetDocuments, Clio, RocketMatter, Centerbase, PracticeMaster, Actionstep, LawBase, etc. All these applications have task lists that allow you to associate tasks with specific matters/projects so when you open the matter/project file, you can see your own and everyone else's tasks in that file. Historically, the problem with these task lists has been that isn't easy to create a task while away from your desk. This has changed tremendously with SaaS applications that have wonderful mobile apps to create & manage tasks. Most of these tools also offer basic synchronization with Outlook.

If you don't have a practice management program and you aren't going to use Microsoft ToDo with Outlook, I would recommend that you explore these options:

1. Microsoft Planner (some integration with Outlook tasks)

2. Microsoft OneNote (some integration with Outlook tasks)

3. Google Tasks

4. OmniFocus

5. Asana

6. Todoist

Chapter 5.

TASK MANAGEMENT—DAILY PLANNING

Now that you have converted emails to tasks and you also have done your "Gathering and Get Organized" session to populate your Master Task List, you are ready to start executing—getting stuff done! For this, you need a game plan. That game plan consists of daily planning (a 5-minute commitment), which is covered in this chapter, and weekly planning, which is covered in the next chapter.

Recall, we always operate and focus better when working from shorter lists. You will always perform better *on a daily basis* if you have a list of 5 things vs. 100 things.

HOW TO CREATE YOUR DAILY PLAN

As a lawyer and consultant who has been paperless for 20+ years, as much as I love technology, I am not ashamed to say that I am a big fan of using paper for daily planning. Take simple index cards as one example. A pack of 100 index cards will cost you less than $3. Use one card per day, writing 3 to 5 tasks that you want to accomplish that day. Another way of articulating this is "Today will be a success if I complete these 3 to 5 tasks." It is okay to re-write items that are on your calendar, and if you get those 3 to 5 things completed, get another card out and write down 3 more tasks.

The Simple Index Card

Simply identify and write 3 to 5 things that you want to focus on and complete.

Tuesday Tasks
1. Enter yesterday's time that I forgot
2. Review prebills
3. VA project (2 hours)
4. Call Sam
5. Research Jones statute of limitations

Tame the Digital Chaos Daily Planning Journal

My favorite option for daily planning is a paper-based planning journal. Again, like index cards, you will keep the plan open and visible all day, probably near your keyboard. Here is an example of my TDC (Tame the Digital Chaos) Daily Planning Journal:

Directions

1. Enter today's date.

2. Identify 3 to 5 tasks that you want to focus on that day. If there are subtasks or notes, use the lines located to the right of the main tasks.

3. Time-block your entire day in 30-minute increments.

4. Enter 3 grateful thoughts.

5. Enter miscellaneous notes or life lessons that day.

Example of completed day:

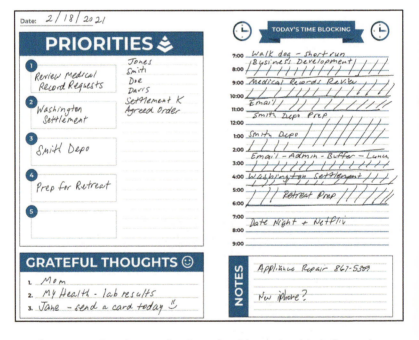

Some people ask me why they should rewrite this information on paper if it is already on the calendar in Outlook. There are multiple reasons:

- Your roadmap for the day should be prominently in front of you so you can always see it. If it is out of sight, it is out of mind. For me, that means that the list is near my keyboard. If the list is in Outlook, it is probably minimized most of the day.

- You don't want to waste a big computer monitor to display your daily plan. Use your monitors for more useful functions like comparing documents or displaying reference/subject matter relevant to projects that you are working on.

- It is possible that events on your calendar were created weeks ago, so they are not fresh on your mind. It is helpful to rewrite those events on the day you plan to work on them.

- Time-blocking those events and tasks helps you engage in realistic planning for your day.

- Taking 5 minutes to write your daily plan serves as a contract with yourself to get those things done that day.

Using your iPad or Tablet

I like my Tame the Digital Chaos journal so much that I created a digital template with it in an app on my iPad called GoodNotes. I then turn off the sleep function on my iPad and keep it plugged in and open on my desk all day. It's just like paper, but more functional—and it doesn't kill any trees.

Microsoft ToDo—My Day

If you don't want to use paper for daily planning, consider **My Day** in Microsoft ToDo. Right-click on a task in Microsoft ToDo and select **Add to My Day**. This will serve as your daily task list. For your time-blocking, use your digital calendar to plan your day in 30-minute increments.

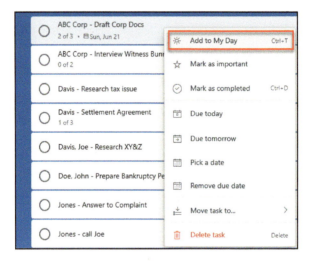

Then at the home screen in Microsoft ToDo, select **My Day** to view your daily task list.

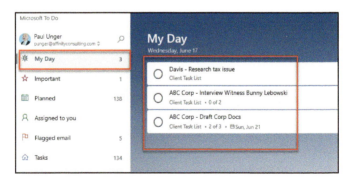

Many people prefer to use a paper-based daily task list because the My Day list tends to get buried or minimized on a computer screen. Additionally, My Day also doesn't have an area for you time-block your day. If it is out of sight, it is out of mind for many people.

The paper-based daily planning journal can sit next to your keyboard and serve as a constant reminder to you to get the short list of 3 to 5 things done.

Chapter 6.

TASK MANAGEMENT—WEEKLY PLANNING

A once-a-week "get organized" deep dive is essential to successful time management and distraction control. This is a once weekly 60-minute commitment to help you frame realistic daily plans, review all tasks and deadlines on your plate, catch up on tasks that "slip between the cracks," and keep you focused on the big picture goals that you want to achieve. It will help you stay driven and will give you the power of creativity and a sense of control in your day and in your life.

HOW TO DO A WEEKLY DEEP DIVE

1. **Do your weekly deep dive planning session on the same day and time each week.** Same time, same place, same channel! Plan 60 minutes for this session, one day per week. Performing this one-hour ritual on the same day and time each week will make it infinitely easier to develop a habit of engaging in this important planning. Moreover, it is proof to your team (and yourself) about how important and sacred this practice is to your organization.

2. **Think about using the "buddy system."** Learning new healthy time management habits is very much like learning new exercise habits. Team up with a colleague and do your own weekly deep-dive planning sessions at the same time. Let me be clear. You are not talking to each other or planning with each other. It is admittedly a little awkward, but just get on the phone or a web meeting and do your own planning in dead silence. In fact, commit *not* to disturb each other.

3. **The Weekly Deep Dive Checklist.** At each weekly planning session, these are all the planning tasks that you will perform:

   ### Weekly Deep Dive Checklist

   ☐ **Review Calendar Two-Weeks Forward.** Open up your calendar and touch every single appointment on your calendar. Stop—pause—think about what you have to do to prepare for the appointment. Can you move forward with it? Do you have to do any research? Do you need to time-block (make an appointment with yourself on your calendar) to prepare? If so, block out your preparation time. If you need to look out further than two weeks, adjust your look-forward time. For example, I look two weeks forward at every appointment, and then I look four additional weeks to find appointments that require travel arrangements, so I can make travel plans (book flights, hotels, rental cars, etc.) in time.

   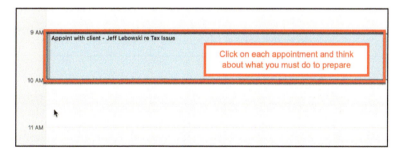

   ☐ **Review Calendar Two-Weeks Back.** Open your calendar and touch every single appointment on your calendar, going two weeks back. Stop—pause—think about whether you did everything that you promised people in those appointments. If not, schedule time to do those things and update your task list.

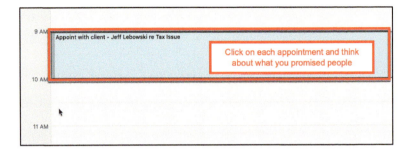

- ☐ **Review your Case/Matter/Project List.** Whether you work with cases, matters, projects, or all of the above, you'd better have a list of all your active cases, matters, and/or projects! If you don't, you absolutely should. Learn how to run reports from your software systems. Some people already do a weekly "case review" on their own or with their team. I used to do mine every Wednesday morning when I was in private practice. That is a different type of meeting than this weekly deep dive. It is an excellent practice and I highly encourage it! However, in that meeting, you *and your team* may dive into the nitty gritty of your cases to get a 500-foot view. In the Weekly Deep Dive, you are only spending about 10 minutes looking at the entire list from a 20,000- or 30,000-foot view. Review the list for the following:

  - Does your list include all new cases, matters, or projects that landed on your plate this week?

  - Can you remove any cases, matters, projects that closed this week?

  - For each item on the list, ask yourself, "Am I on track or off track?" If you are off track, block off 15-30 or 60 minutes on your calendar to do a deep dive into that case, matter, or project. Do not stop your weekly deep dive into work on the project.

- ☐ **Review your Task List and Follow-Up Email Folder.** Review each and every item on your task list.

Stop—pause—really think about each item. Just like with the calendar, above, you are *not* skimming. You are thinking about each item. Ask yourself:

- Is the task complete? If so, mark it complete.

- Is the task still relevant? If not, delete it.

- Is the task overdue, urgent, or about to become urgent? If so, block off time on your calendar to get it done!

- Do you need to provide a status update to anyone?

- Do you need to follow-up with anyone in order for you to complete this task? Are you waiting on someone else?

- Finally, and this is important, remember to check all of your task lists, including any "Someday" or "Bucket" lists. We too often forget to check our strategic planning or quarterly or long-term lists and then these items never get done! It is vital that we have a routine/system in place that makes us review all items on all task lists.

☐ **Batch Process Email (Delete, Delegate, and Delay).** Process your inbox to **Delete** any emails that you can. Then, **Delegate** any emails you need to. Finally, if you need to **Delay** acting on an email, be sure to record it on your task list, create an appointment with yourself to do it (time block), and then save the email into the case/matter/project folder so you can delete it from your inbox. Remember, your inbox is a terrible task list. I know that I have already stated this, but I will say it again (and probably more)—stop using your inbox as a task list!

Note: You will note that I removed the **Do** from 4 D's during the weekly deep dive (you typically Delete, Do, Delegate, and Delay). This omission was intentional. If you do the "Do" during the weekly deep dive, it will not take you just 60 minutes to complete; it will take you all day. For the weekly deep dive, just focus on Delete, Delegate, and Delay.

Remember also, if you use Outlook, you can easily convert emails to tasks by dragging and dropping an email on to the Task icon in Outlook or use Quick Steps.

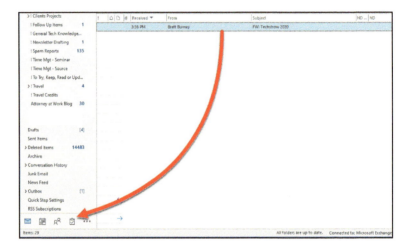

This function acts as a "copy" and will create a task, while still leaving the email in your inbox for you to take further action like creating a calendar event or filing it away. You can convert that same email to an appointment by dragging it on to your Calendar icon.

- ☐ **Clean your Desk, Piles, Stickies, and Notes**. During the week as life happens, it would be ideal to enter all tasks and do all your time blocking on your calendar immediately as tasks surface. We all know that this isn't the way it happens sometimes. You may be running out the door when the phone rings and someone asks you to do something. So, you quickly jot it down on a sticky note and slap it on your desk or computer monitor. Likewise, maybe someone dropped off a pile of paper that is sitting on your desk. All these things need processed or checked in. They are tasks and appointments that should be entered into your system and then you should scan and save those papers and throw away the sticky notes. The end result is that (1) you have a single place where you need to look & manage your tasks (not 10 or 20 notes, stickies, piles, etc.), and (2) you have a clean desk, which will help you focus.

☐ **Weekly Time Report.** Review your billable timesheets for the week. Learn how to run a report from your time billing and accounting system (or have someone run it for you). For this information, again, stop, pause, and think about each time entry and ask yourself:

- o Did I do everything that I promised relating to the activity that I performed for this time entry? If not, update your task list and/or schedule time on your calendar to do it.

- o Are there any follow-up items that I should pursue relating to this time entry?

- o Is there any potential new business or opportunities that I have overlooked? If so, add it to your task list and your calendar.

By performing this weekly ritual, you kill three birds with one stone:

1. You proof your time entries for typos, grammar, and accuracy, preventing you from having to do a massive review once a month.

2. You are reminded of tasks that you need to perform that you failed to do.

3. You will also stumble across time entries that you forgot to enter, thereby billing more time, and who doesn't want that?

Here is a quick summary of all 7 things to do during your Weekly Deep Dive.

- ✅ Calendar – 2 weeks Forward
- ✅ Calendar – 2 weeks Back
- ✅ Project/Case List
- ✅ Task List <u>and</u> Follow-Up Folder
- ✅ Email (Delete, Delegate, Delay)
- ✅ Loose Papers & Notes
- ✅ Time Report (1 week back)

Chapter 7.

OUTLOOK ESSENTIALS FOR BETTER TIME, TASK, AND EMAIL MANAGEMENT

INTRODUCTION

Having a fundamental understanding of how Outlook works (or whatever email and calendaring system you use, *i.e.*, Gmail, Clio, etc.) is vital to your success with time, task, and email management. Depending on the industry, 75–95% of the business world uses Outlook for email and calendaring. It is the gold standard. For this reason, I am going to focus on essential Outlook features that will help you manage your time. If you use one of the other platforms, don't skip this chapter. Nearly all the functions found here are present in those systems, too. In fact, it is fair to say that most of those systems have used Outlook as the model to build their own. If you use another system, look for these features within your system.

INBOX TOOLS FOR BETTER ORGANIZATION

Storage and Organization Problems with Email

- **Disorganization:** Most people have hundreds or thousands of unrelated messages in their inboxes. This is equivalent to taking all of the paper out of your files and throwing it on the floor of the file room. The point is, if it's not organized, then it's mostly useless. I know that Outlook and other tools have a search function, but that just isn't a good way to store documents and email. As people providing professional services to individuals, businesses, or business units, we must be able to see and quickly locate all emails that are part of the same project, matter, or case.

- **Storage Space Limitations:** You may have been scolded by your IT folks about this. If you're using Microsoft Exchange on your server, then it can get overloaded with the quantity of emails and attachments you keep in your inbox and Outlook folder structures. If you don't have Exchange, then all of those emails (and contacts, appointments, and tasks) are stored in a PST file on your local hard drive or possibly the organization's server. The bigger that database, the slower your computer will run. Of course, the database can also over-run your storage capacity.

- **No One Else Can See Your Email But You:** In most cases, if you have important client communication in Outlook, no one else in your office can see it. In many cases, we want to share this information, but don't know how to do it.

- **Difficulties Searching:** Many people complain that it's nearly impossible to efficiently search old emails for a particular conversation. What can you do to make searching easier?

Set Up Folders to Organize Your Inbox

To preface this discussion, if you work with a team of people, creating subfolders under your inbox may trap emails in a place where no one else can see those emails. There are tools that solve this problem. For instance, within document management systems (DMS) like Worldox, NetDocuments, and iManage, you can map these subfolders to matter or project folders that exist in the document management program. Any emails saved into those subfolders are automatically uploaded into the matter in the DMS where others on your team have access to them. If you have a DMS, it is fine to create subfolders if you use that feature. If you have Microsoft 365, your mailbox capacity is fairly large, so running out of space should not become a problem as long as you are regularly archiving closed projects and matters.

If you do not have a DMS *and* you work with a team of people, creating inbox subfolders can create problems for everyone on the team who needs to see those emails. It usually results in people not having access to critical information, and lots of duplicate emails getting forwarded. The best solution to this problem is a document management system. If you don't need to worry about sharing email communication with other team members, go ahead and create subfolders to organize those emails.

To create subfolders within your inbox (or another folder), right click the inbox (or your mailbox) > **New Folder**. Give it a name and click **OK**.

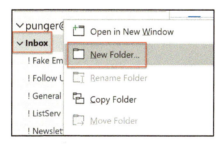

If you have a document management system, you can take the next step to map that inbox subfolder to the matter or case so everyone in the office will be able to see the emails that you drag into that folder. In NetDocuments, for example, Right-click on the inbox subfolder and select **Map Folder to ND**.

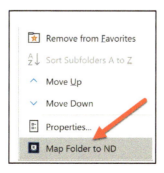

Outlook Rule—Auto Route Email to Subfolder

Many times, we want Outlook to automatically perform a function based on certain criteria or a situation. For instance, if you get 50 emails a day from a listserv or an association, you may want to automatically route the emails into a specific subfolder. An Outlook rule can help you with this situation. Here are the steps:

1. Find an email in your inbox folder from the listserv, person or entity. Right-click on the email.

2. Select **Rules > Create Rule**.

3. Select the conditions to trigger the rule and the desired folder, and **OK**.

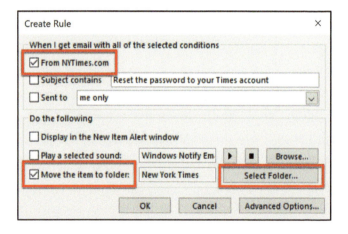

Once the Outlook Rule is created, any emails that would otherwise land in your inbox will be automatically routed to your special folder. It will not clutter your inbox and you will not have to process those. When you want to look at them or find an email within them, simply navigate to that folder and either read through them or run a search.

Outlook Rule—Notify Me of Emails from Very Important People (VIPs)

As discussed above, I generally recommend that people turn off Outlook email notifications to avoid distractions throughout the day. However, we do want interruptions from certain important people in our lives. These might be special clients, a mentor, a colleague, partner, or loved ones. An Outlook rule can alert us for these special people. Here are the steps:

1. Find an email from that special person in your inbox or deleted items folder. Right-click on the email.

2. Select **Rules** > **Create Rule**.

3. Select the conditions to trigger the rule and the desired folder:

    a. When it is from {a particular person}

    b. Display a New Item Alert window; and

    c. Play a selected sound

4. **OK** to save the changes.

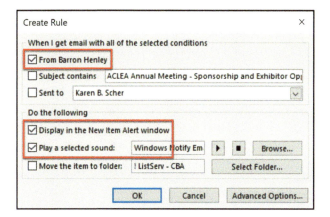

Outlook Rule—Delay Delivery by 1 Minute

Many times, you hit **Send** and then 2 seconds later you have a Homer Simpson moment and realize that you forgot to include someone or you realize that you sent it to the wrong person. If you do this often, you may want to create a rule in Outlook that gives you a buffer period to go edit the email from your outbox. Here is how:

1. In Outlook, click on the **File** tab > Manage Rules and Alerts > **New Rule** button.

2. Under "**Start from a Blank Rule**," choose "**Apply Rule on Messages that I Send**" and hit **Next**.

3. On the next screen ("which conditions do you want to check"), don't check anything (you want this rule to apply to every email you send) and click the **Next** button at the bottom. You'll see the following dialog (click **Yes**):

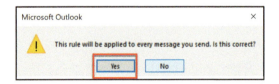

4. On the next screen, check "**defer delivery by a number of minutes**," and then click the hyperlink for "a number of" at the bottom of the screen and enter the number of minutes you want to delay your email. I suggest **1 minute**.

5. Click **Next** and add any exceptions (probably none for this rule).

6. Click **Next**, name your rule "Delay by 1 minute" and click **Finish**.

Outlook Rules—Managing, Editing, Deleting, Turning On or Off

You may want to delete, edit, or temporarily turn off a rule from time to time. For instance, if you have an all-day meeting, or a big trial tomorrow, you may decide to completely ghost everyone and cut yourself off from the world to prepare. This is essential to do on occasion. You may want to turn off the special notifications that you get from your "VIP" list. To do this, select the **File** tab > **Manage Rules and Alerts**.

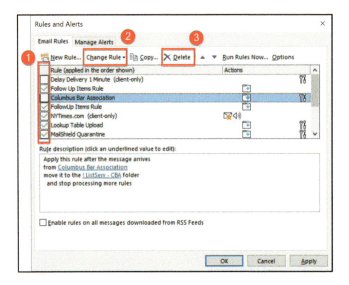

1. Check or Uncheck appropriate boxes to turn them ON or OFF.

2. Select Change Rule to edit rule.

3. Select Delete to delete a rule.

Conditional Formatting to Apply Colors to Special Emails

Sometimes you may want to automatically apply color to an important email or when it is from a particular sender. This is *not* done with an Outlook rule. Instead, you use a feature called conditional formatting.

Here are the Steps:

1. In Outlook email, go to the **View** ribbon. Select **View Settings**. Next, select **Conditional Formatting**.

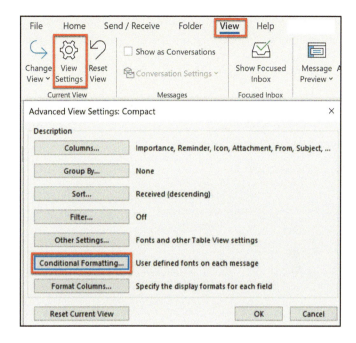

2. Select **Add** and give it a name. I called mine below "Barron Henley" because I want all emails from Barron Henley to turn RED in the desired font. Next, select the **Font** button to select the desired font, color & size.

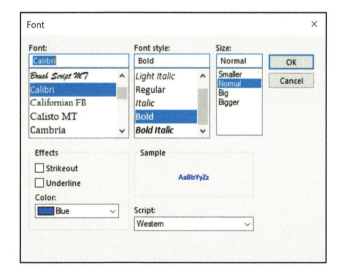

3. Select the **Condition** button. You can set your own condition. In this case, the **From** field should indicate the Sender's name. You could do something else such as all emails where the subject line contains "ABA."

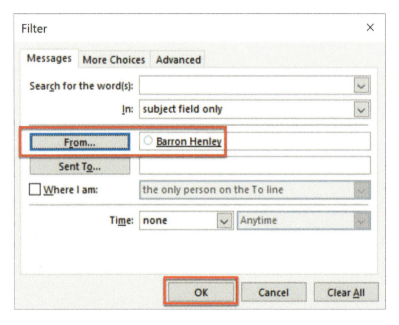

Click **OK**, and now the conditional formatting will be applied to all emails in your inbox.

Flagging Email

I have mixed feelings about using flags in Outlook's email. I fear that using this technique may encourage people to use the inbox and its subfolders as a task list (which is something that I adamantly oppose, and I discussed above).

However, if you process your inbox down to zero every day and the volume of email that you receive is relatively low, flags may be a good tool for some people. Flags can alert you to follow up on an important task or email. Simply right click on the desired email and select **Follow Up** and then select the desired follow-up flag. By flagging an email, the email will automatically show up on your To Do list in Outlook, but they also stay in your inbox.

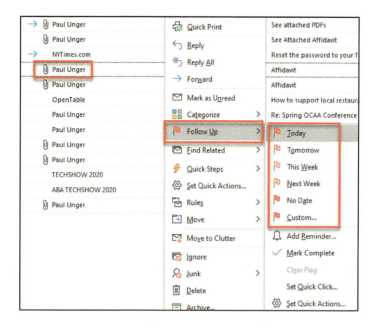

You can set a custom flag with a date as well. Outlook will notify you on the date and time specified.

Personally, I rarely ever use flags with email. Some people who don't get a large volume of emails use them all the time. It is ultimately your choice. It is an available tool, so I wanted to at least show it to you so you can decide for yourself if it would be helpful or hurtful.

Outlook Views

Many people complain that the Outlook interface is too complicated. To simplify the end-user interface, and see more emails in a single screen, you can try a few things:

1. **Turn Off Date Grouping.** By default, Outlook groups your email by date received. To many, the date groupings just occupy space and prevent you from seeing all of your email on one screen. To turn it off, click the **View** tab > expand the Arrangement box via the drop-down button > **Arrangement** > uncheck **Show in Groups**.

2. **Turn Off Message Preview Lines.** By default, Outlook has preview lines turned on. Many feel this makes the email list look cluttered and hard to read. Others love it.

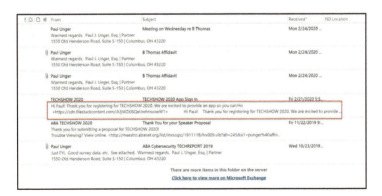

To turn off Preview Lines, click the **View** tab > **Message Preview** > and then **Off**.

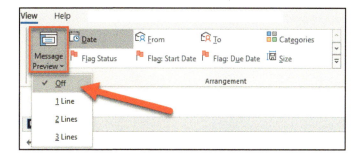

3. Turn **Off Reading Pane**. Many people like the reading pane (including me), but if you don't, this occupies a lot of screen space that could otherwise be displaying email. To turn it off, click the **View** tab > **Reading Pane** > **Off**.

Out of Office Assistant

There are times when you need to put the world on notice that you are not available to answer emails. This could be because of vacation or a big project. Use this sparingly. You do not want to send the wrong message to your clients that you are always unavailable. You also don't want to unnecessarily clutter people's inboxes with your autoreplies. That can be very annoying if over-used. To set up automatic replies:

1. Select the **File** tab > and then **Automatic Replies**.

2. Set a time range for the automatic reply.

3. Type the desired automatic reply text for inside and outside your organization and click **OK**.

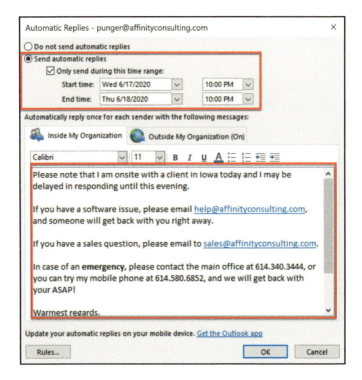

Signatures

Signatures are helpful to automate the insertion of signature blocks. Many use it to insert other snippets of text (like the functionality of AutoText entries or Email Templates).

1. In Outlook, click the **File** tab > **Options** button > **Mail** tab (left side) > **Signatures** button.

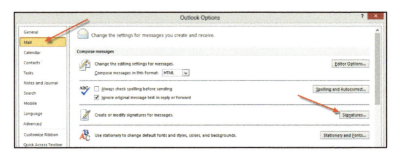

2. Select **New**, name your signature and then type (or paste) the desired text in your text field (bottom pane). Click **OK** when finished.

3. You may want to create a signature for New messages and a different one for Replies.

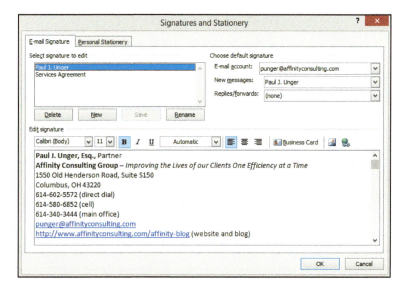

If you set up alternative signatures or text snippets to insert, you can insert those "signatures" within the email by right-clicking next to your existing signature. Your alternative signatures or text snippets will appear. Select the desired option to insert and the text will be inserted.

You may also insert the signatures from the **Message** tab within the email.

Archiving Email

Many Outlook users end up with an enormous accumulation of email in their Sent Mail and Deleted Mail folders. Furthermore, some mail is sorted into subfolders and forgotten about. All of this will start to bog down Outlook's performance as those databases of emails get larger and larger. Thankfully, Outlook has a way of dealing with this problem via **AutoArchive**.

In a nutshell, AutoArchive will allow you to (a) permanently delete, (b) delete, or (c) archive old or expired items to an archive file (archived database). Conveniently, the first time AutoArchive runs, it creates the archive database for you. It is stored on the C drive by default so you'll either want to move it to a server folder or back it up directly from your C drive. Once it has established itself, you'll see the Archive folder in your Outlook Folder List.

To Turn AutoArchive On or Off on a Specific Folder:

You can control what any particular folder does in Outlook by following these steps: Right-click the desired folder > choose **Properties** > click the **AutoArchive** tab > Make your changes and click **OK**.

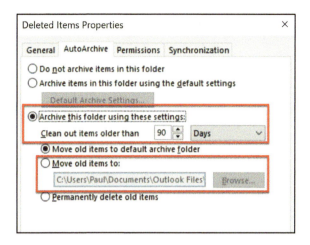

Quick Steps

Quick steps are used to automate repetitive steps. You can apply multiple actions in one-click, or fewer clicks, to email messages. This helps you quickly manage your mailbox. As an example, if you frequently move messages to a specific folder, you can use a Quick Step to move the message in one- click. To create a quick step, click **Create New** in the Quick Steps gallery. Choose the steps to repeat. This will create a button that will execute those steps. Here are a few very common workflows that would be perfect for creating a Quick Step.

Quick Step—Send Email to Multiple Recipients

1. Click "Create New" in the Quick Step gallery.

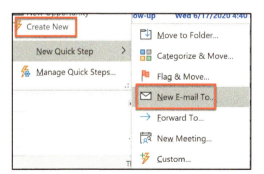

2. Select New Email To.

3. Give the Quick Step a Name.

4. Add the desired Recipients in the **To** field.

5. Select **Finish**.

The Quick Step is now available to use from the **Home** tab. When executed, it will automatically create a new message to all the intended recipients.

Quick Step—Convert Email to Appointment and Move to a Folder

For this Quick Step, we are going to combine 2 actions. Note that you can have Outlook perform more than 2 actions. I am unaware of a limit, but I have some Quick Steps performing 3 or 4 actions, and it is all kicked off with a single-click.

Click "Create New" in the Quick Step gallery > select **Custom**.

1. Give the Quick Step a Name.

2. Add the first Action—Create an appointment with attachment.

3. Add the second Action—Move to folder > then select the desired folder.

4. Add any additional desired Action.

5. Assign a Shortcut key, if desired.

6. Add any Tooltip text, if desired.

7. Select Finish.

Chapter 8.

THE "NOT TO-DO LIST" - YOUR 26 WEEK PLAN

In the chapters above, I outline many strategies to manage tasks and distractions. However, I thought it might be helpful to help you assemble an Action Plan and state them a slightly different way . . . as a "NOT to do list." Here are 26 "Nots" over 26 weeks to keep yourself laser focused.

DON'T TRY TO BOIL THE OCEAN!

Focus on each item one week at a time. Go out of order if you want. You make the rules and can tweak the processes in this book as needed. While one item per week may not seem fast enough for you, let me assure you, if you are following 80% of these rules 6 months from now, you will be in great shape. Have a little patience and execute each item consistently. Think of the long game. When you feel ready, move on to another item. If you want to go *a little* faster, go ahead. Be an overachiever. If you stumble, just stop and regroup. Take a week or two and focus on the items that you have already executed. Don't take on a new item until you are comfortably back on the wagon.

PREPARE & CARE FOR YOUR BRAIN

☑ **Week 1 - Do NOT Neglect Sleep!**

Insomnia was a problem before Covid-19. It is no surprise that Covid-19 has piled on even more reasons to lose sleep: stress, "cabin fever," anxiety, depression, unemployment, death of loved ones. The list is endless. "It's a problem everywhere, across all age groups," ... "the increase [of insomnia] is enormous," said Angela Drake, a UC Davis Health clinical professor in the Department of Psychiatry.

According to the U.S. Centers for Disease Control and Prevention and the National Sleep Foundation (www.cdc.gov/sleep), most healthy adults need 7–9 hours of sleep per night. Good sleep quality is very important. Getting up several times a night or waking up multiple times per night with breathing problems can adversely affect the quality of your sleep.

According to research at the University of Toronto, even just one night of sleep deprivation showed significant decline in cognitive performance. fMRI studies showed declined activity in certain regions of the prefrontal cortex, the same area of the brain that allow for decision-making, problem-solving and planning (Front. Hum. Neurosci., 22 April 2014).

WebMD states that poor sleep leads to significant problems, some of which are very serious:

- Moodiness
- Anxiousness
- Paranoia
- Depressed mood
- Difficulty understanding new concepts
- Forgetfulness
- Lack of focus
- High blood pressure
- Severe headaches
- Diabetes

Dr. Drake from UC Davis provides these tips for better sleep:

1. Keep a normal routine of sleep.
2. Start a going-to-bed routine.
3. Avoid computer & TV screens in the bedroom.
4. Don't use your bedroom as your office.
5. Exercise during the day.
6. Don't take naps during the day over 10 minutes.
7. Get exposure to sunlight.
8. Don't eat dinner late or late snacks.
9. If you wake up in the middle of the night and can't go back to sleep, get out of bed.

10. Cut back on news and social media in the evening.
11. Go easy on alcohol and caffeine.
12. Meditate using one of the many apps available.

(*UC Davis Health*, Newsroom, September 23, 2020)

☑ Week 2 - Do NOT Worry So Much!

"Worrying doesn't take away tomorrow's troubles. It takes away today's peace."

- Unknown

Worrying can be good, but not when it is excessive. For instance, if you have a presentation tomorrow in front of your peers, or a hearing before a new judge, a little bit of "healthy" worrying can be extremely helpful so you can prepare. On one hand, your worries can make you and your organization more prepared for situations. On the other hand, when your worrying is excessive, it can be annoying and even outright paralyzing. It can bring projects to a complete halt.

The science behind worrying is fascinating. The same circuits in the frontal lobes of your brain that allow for superior human intelligence: decision-making, problem-solving, and planning, are also responsible for worry & anxiety. When higher-functioning brain regions are preoccupied with worry, you can't access them for the other things like decision-making, etc. Worrying takes precedent. When this happens, your amygdala hijacks your brain and puts the brakes on higher-level thinking.

Further, according to the Chopra Center (www.chopra.com), worrying too much can affect both mind <u>and</u> body:

- Disrupted sleep
- Headaches
- Concentration difficulties
- Nausea
- Muscle tension
- Exhaustion
- Irritability

- Elevated cortisol (stress hormone)
- Difficulty making decisions

Breaking the cycle of worry can be difficult but let me share with you two practical strategies that help me.

First, practice mindfulness or another form of meditation. If you are unfamiliar, I strongly recommend a few apps to try on your smartphone that will lead you through short, but very helpful sessions:

- Headspace
- Breathe
- Calm

Second, start a journal to write down those things that are worrying you, and then get back to the work at hand. Also use the journal before you go to bed to write down how you feel. Many times, putting it down on paper can bring clarity. At a minimum, it will reduce anxiety. I write down micro-entries (very short bullet points) in my daily planning journal. It requires 1-2 minutes of my time.

☑ Week 3 – Do NOT Doomscroll or Doomsurf

Do you ever find yourself unable to put your device down, as you scroll through the infinite number of social media posts on Facebook and the like? Most of it is either bad news or someone painting their lives as perfect with their perfect white picket fence, perfect new job promotion, and perfect 6-pack abs after "working out 365 perfect straight days!" Right? It's downright defeating. What are we looking for anyway? Some ray of hope? The reality is that it is not only a huge time-suck, but it is harmful to our mental health. What can you do?

- **Set Boundaries**: I found during the last presidential campaign season that I had to put limits on my exposure to certain politicians and my use of Facebook. For me, it wasn't enough to set aspirational boundaries, I had to utilize

the iOS Screen Time function to block myself from trying to knock some cyber sense into some of my family and friends because they did not share the same political and moral beliefs. With Screen Time (and similar functions on an Android device), you can completely block yourself from apps during desired hours, and you can limit your total time to however much time you designate. For instance, no more than 30 minutes a day on Facebook.
- **Replace Doomscrolling with Something Healthy**: If during business hours, anytime you feel the urge to jump on Facebook, instead dedicate that time to reaching out to a colleague or client to check in on them. If during non-business hours, write a letter, card or text message to a family member, or jump on a video call with them. Read a book, go for a walk or run, do pushups, stretch, journal, or clean out a closet.

☑ Week 4 - Do NOT Ruminate – Learn to Tame "Monkey Mind"

Rumination is the process of continuously thinking the same negative thoughts. It occurs during the day, as well as during bouts of insomnia. When some ruminate, they also self-reflect and problem-solve. That sometimes lures people into believing they are doing something healthy or productive.

Related to rumination, but a bit different is "Monkey Mind," or racing thoughts. Where rumination is someone thinking about the same negative thought, Monkey Mind is someone thinking about many different thoughts. For example, you are working late, and you wish you took that job in Canada, which reminds you that you may want to buy a Thermador, but which one and you don't have the money. You next start thinking about cooking classes instead, which reminds you of your ex's terrible cooking, and how you have to fix that nagging roof leak. These thoughts are typically negative as well, and they are all over the place – like a monkey swinging from limb to limb. It is worried, unsettled mental chatter. We sometimes call it catastrophic thinking because nothing goes well, and it usually results in stress over unresolved problems.

Like worrying, fear and jealousy, rumination and monkey mind activates, you guessed it the prefrontal cortex, the part of the brain that is also associated with logical thinking.

Mindfulness. Practicing mindfulness quiets the amygdala, which reduces the release of cortisol. Mindfulness is a form of meditation that often involves deep breathing. It is an incredibly important tool because once the emotions are triggered, we need a practical strategy to stop the racing. To learn about these techniques, I recommend either a therapist, life coach, group meditation, or if none of those appeal to you, there are numerous apps that will privately lead your through these exercises like Headspace, Calm, or Breathe (discussed above).

Rumination Diary. Equally important is learning the environmental triggers and figuring out how to manage them. Many experts recommend keeping a journal to record when it happened, what happened right before the ruminations started, how did it make you feel, what were your thoughts, what stopped it? I found this to be extremely enlightening and discovered that 99% of the time, my monkey mind followed the same 2 triggering events. Once you understand this, you can think about how to manage those triggering events.

If Causing Insomnia, Get out of Bed. If rumination is preventing you from falling asleep, it is important to get out of bed calmly and go do something like light reading or even meditation. Journaling your thoughts is often recommended, even at night. Stay away from bright light or activity that will keep you falling back asleep. Once calm and the rumination stops, try to return to bed.

Positive Talk + Time Limit. You can also combat negative thoughts with racing positive thoughts. You should try to think positive thoughts about yourself, but if you can't, think of other positive thoughts. This lessens the likelihood that we begin to obsess over the negative in the first place. Whatever the case, set a time limit of 10 minutes – not a second longer. After the 10 minutes is up, say to yourself "no thank you, I have already thought about this enough. It is time for peace."

☑ Week 5 - Do NOT Go Without Deep Breathing

One part of mindfulness that I find incredibly helpful is deep breathing (typically 6 breaths per minute). Many promote a 3-count while inhaling, a 3-count hold, and a 3-count while exhaling, but I have seen small variations of this work just as well. While I talk about this topic several times in this chapter, it is so important, inexpensive, and easy that I wanted to dedicate a full week for you to explore and perfect the practice. Perhaps start with deep breathing, and if you like the results, think about mindfulness or another form of meditation.

A 2017 study published in *Frontiers in Psychology* showed that deep breathing resulted in significant improvement on attention, stress and cortisol levels. Deep breathing calms the amygdala, which reduces the secretion of cortisol (see https://www.ncbi.nlm.nih.gov/pmc/articles/PMC5455070/).

☑ Week 6 - Do NOT Neglect Your Brain by Feeding it Poor Nutrition

We too often fill our bodies with unhealthy food that can impair our ability to focus. In the short term, we can experience a food coma after eating too heavily at lunch or consuming too much sugar when snacking. It leaves our brains foggy. In the long term, we may develop chronic diseases that limit our activities and enjoyment of life.

An easy way to achieve better nutrition is by implementing a handful of healthy boundaries. Here are some examples of healthy food boundaries that will lead to weight loss and healthier lifestyle, without having to commit to a formal diet. Adjust these examples to help you control some of your own vices.

- I will not consume more than one 3 oz bag of potato chips per day.
- I will not consume more than 250 calories of sugary snacks.
- I will not eat after 7:00 pm.

- I will always eat a single serving of plain oatmeal for breakfast Monday through Friday.
- I will not consume more than 1800 calories in a single day.
- I will eat no more than 1 small bowl of ice cream per week.
- My dietary intake will be 90% plant-based and 10% animal protein.
- I will replace 90% of my current unhealthy snacks with fruits and nuts.
- I will drink no less than 12 glasses of water per day.

GIVE YOUR BRAIN A SENSE OF CONTROL

When you feel in control, it calms the amygdala and stress response. This is why we always feel more focused and less stressed when we have a plan.

☑ Week 7 - Do NOT Begin Your Day Without a Plan

Instead of jumping into email, begin your day by operating from your daily roadmap. Commit to a 5-minute planning session with yourself at the end of the today for tomorrow or start your day with a 5-minute planning session. If you don't have a plan, you very well may become part of someone else's plan!

Use the Tame the Digital Chaos daily planning sheet, or another commercial planner like Best Self Journal or Panda, for this and time block your day on paper, remembering to state some 30,000-foot goals for the day. Blank planning sheets are included at the end of this book. Recite 3 things that you are thankful for. Put a plan together for your day before diving into email. You can always adjust as the day unfolds but start with a plan! Consider doing your plan at the end of the previous day and spend a couple minutes in the morning reviewing it instead of jumping into email. Also be sure to cross things off from your list as you complete them to give your brain a shot of feel-good dopamine.

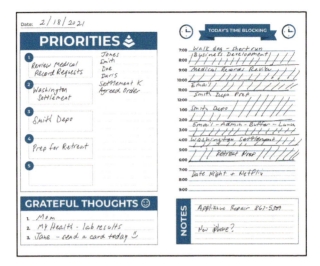

☑ Week 8 - Do NOT Start Your Day Without a Team Huddle

Instead of diving right into your email or your first appointment or project, after your 5-minute daily planning session (above), have a quick huddle with your immediate team. We call this the "lightning round." Each person has 60 seconds to recite what they have going on that day in detail, and broadly for the rest of the week. This encourages communication and awareness of projects, and almost always results in shifting some tasks and schedules around to better distribute work and help each other. It also reduced interruptions during the day because everyone is more aware of deadlines around the team.

If your team works from home or multiple locations, use tools like Zoom, Microsoft Teams, or GoToMeeting. Be disciplined about time. Beware of "meeting creep." If the meetings constantly go over, it is no longer a huddle, and people will quickly grow annoyed. Larger teams should think about breaking into smaller huddles, so this doesn't turn into a 30-minute meeting.

Week 9 - Do NOT Begin Your Week Without Weekly Planning

A once-a-week "get organized" deep dive is absolutely essential to successful time and distraction management. This is a 60-minute commitment once a week. It will help you frame realistic daily planning, clean your workspace, eliminate piles, review all tasks and deadlines on your plate, catch up on tasks that slip between the cracks, and keep focused on the big picture goals that you want to achieve. It will help you stay driven. Failing to plan is planning to fail.

It is extremely helpful do your weekly deep dive planning session on the same day and time each week. Performing this one-hour ritual on the same day and time each week will make it infinitely easier to develop a habit of engaging in this important planning.

Try to do your deep-dive 2 to 3 days before starting the next week.

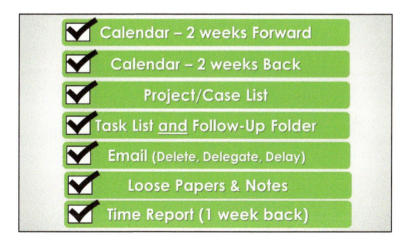

Week 10 - Do NOT Fail to Write Down Tasks and Random Neural Firings

The main reason tasks and deadlines slip between the cracks is because people fail to immediately write them down in an organized system. The reason they do not enter them into an organized system is because they are too cumbersome to record, especially when they are not at their computer.

The answer to this problem is an application like Microsoft ToDo. ToDo is available on your PC, Mac, Tablet, iPad, iPhone, Android Phone, and on the web. No matter where you enter or edit an item on that list, it updates it everywhere else. Most importantly, it is a beautifully designed program that it easy to use:

To add icing on the cake, Microsoft ToDo integrates seamlessly with Microsoft Outlook. Any task that you create in one application will be created in the other.

☑ Week 11 - Do NOT Keep 20 Different Lists

Having tasks in too many locations is a major faux pas. If you have to look in 20 different places for information or tasks, you are bound to miss something. Consolidate and simplify your lists. Microsoft ToDo is a great solution for this problem because you can create and organize your lists very easily. Keep your task lists simple. Here is how that looks in Microsoft ToDo:

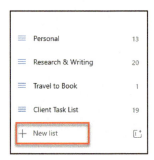

Week 12 - Do NOT Use Poor Descriptions in Your Task Lists!

When you read descriptions in your task list, are they vague? Do you know exactly what you need to do next? Here is a common example of a task list that I see when I do one-on-one coaching:

- Work on the Smith Case

- Jones Hearing

- Davis Settlement

- Joe's Annual Evaluation

While you may have known what these descriptions meant when you wrote them, (1) none of them articulate exactly what action you must do next, and (2) chances are if you know what those next steps are right now, you probably will forget those details by tomorrow or the next day. One of the primary reasons why we procrastinate is because we do not know that next step or where we left off.

Using one of the examples above, I can't start Joe's Annual Evaluation until I receive his HR information from Anne and I get Joe's self-evaluation. So, a better way to record the task is to provide the details of the next steps. This is how that would look in a task list like Microsoft ToDo:

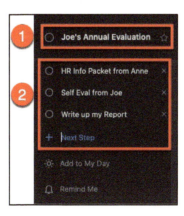

1. Main Task Description

2. Steps or Subtasks with Detail

☑ Week 13 - Do NOT Underutilize Your Calendar

Many people simply leave tasks, deadlines, and ticklers in their task list and set up "Reminders." While that works for some people, it doesn't work for the majority of people. Having a task on a task list is vital because it stays there until it is marked complete. However, if it is 1 of 100 other tasks, it might get lost in the weeds. Scheduling time to work on the task on your calendar is critical because you can see it clearly on a particular date. That date may be the date that it is due, or the date that you are blocking off time to work on it. Having the task in both places is important because if you fail to get something done on a certain day and it is only recorded on the calendar, you may fail to remember to do that task unless you go back and look at a previous date. If it is on your task list also, it will still be there as unresolved. This dual system is key for certain tasks that have deadlines. I don't think it is essential for all types of tasks. For instance, I would rarely, if ever, put "buy milk and eggs" on my calendar. However, if I must have a contract drafted by a certain date, I will most likely have that in my task list, in my calendar on the date that it is due, and in my calendar as an appointment with myself to work on it.

There are three categories of events that people fail to record on their calendar:

- Time Blocking - appointments with yourself to do a task.

- Ticklers - reminders to check in with someone or see if you received something from someone.

- Deadlines - hard deadlines for a project or deliverable (*e.g.*, draft a contract for the Davis case).

The bottom line is that we must get in the habit of recording tasks *and* scheduling deadlines *and* block off time to perform that work on our calendar.

Example—Opinion Letter on § 501(c)(3) Status of ABC Corp. This is DUE on December 1, 2020 to the client. What entries might you want to make?

- Record the task in Microsoft ToDo with the DUE DATE and a reminder 3 days before at 9 am. "ABC Corp - Opinion Letter" with all needed details in the steps or notes section. (TASK ON TASK LIST).

- Create an appointment in Outlook on December 1 at 9 am: "ABC Corp - Opinion Letter DUE to Alex Smith" (DEADLINE ON CALENDAR). You may also want to record needed deadlines within any firm-required systems, like a practice management program or a docketing system.

- Create an appointment in Outlook on November 17th from 2–5 pm to work on Opinion Letter (TIME BLOCKING).

- Create an appointment in Outlook on November 26th from 3–5 pm to finalize Opinion Letter. (TIME BLOCKING)

- Create an Appointment on November 13th to check in with associate Barb on the status of her research and opinion letter (TICKLER).

MANAGE DISTRACTIONS

☑ Week 14 - Do NOT Keep Your Outlook Inbox Up on Your Computer Monitor All Day

Stop checking your inbox 70+ times a day! Your inbox is one of the most disruptive tools if you are trying to focus on project work, billable work, or deep level work. It's like choosing to write a complex brief or letter in a war zone or a nursery full of screaming children. Literally every 2 to 3 minutes, a bomb is landing in your inbox. How can one possibly focus while working in an environment like that? Instead, skim your calendar in the morning and decide how many times and for how long you can batch process your emails that day. Every day will be different. Aim for something reasonable like 5 times a day (the average worker checks email an idiotic 74 times a day!).

Be more deliberate about when you check email by batch processing email, following the 3-minute rule and the 4 Ds. For instance, instead of checking email 74 times a day, you may only check it 5 times a day:

Today's Batch Email Processing	
7:30 AM	15 minutes
10:00 AM	30 minutes
12 Noon	90 minutes
4:00 pm	30 minutes
5:00 pm	15 minutes

Use your dual monitors to display documents or information that is relevant to the work that you are performing, not your inbox.

☑ Week 15 - Do NOT Turn on Notifications

We all should be aware of the perilous cost of task-switching. Notifications are invitations to task-switch. They are like a dozen little devils sitting on our shoulder, tempting us to do everything except what we are supposed to be doing, and those devils have a direct hotline to our brain. Why would we give the world a hotline to our brain? Turn all notifications off—and I mean ALL of them, including those on your smartphones. In Outlook, email notifications can be turned off by navigating to **File > Options > Mail** and deselecting the four different methods of notifying you when a new message arrives.

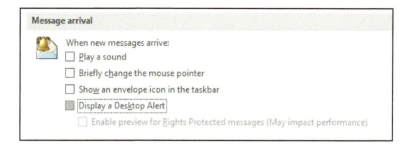

☑ Week 16 - Do NOT Answer All Calls as They Come In

We never want to miss an important call, but you one must balance this with work that needs to be finished. If your job is sales/business development, you probably will take more calls as they come in, even from unknown callers. If your job is mostly project work, you should answer fewer calls as they come in. If you have a receptionist or use service like Smith AI virtual receptionists (www.smith.ai) Ruby Receptionists (www.ruby.com), perhaps they can field and filter these distractions. When we take all calls as they come in, we also run the risk of derailing our day by getting sucked into a conversation that we aren't prepared to resolve. It is always a little dangerous. Retrieve the message, do any needed research, and then call the person back in a timely manner with all the needed answers. Batch return telephone calls, just like we should do with emails.

☑ Week 17 - Do NOT Multitask!

It is not enough to say that multitasking is bad. We need to practice single tasking. We need to clear our desks *and* our multiple monitors of information that is not directly relevant to the project that we are executing. One way to do this is using the Pomodoro Technique®. Pomodoro is an easy technique that utilizes the 25-minute tomato timer. You single-task (preferably deep-level work/project work) for 25 minutes and then take a break and do whatever we want for 5 minutes. In other words, we work in intervals. The human brain functions very well maintaining attention to a single task for 25 minutes. After 25 minutes, we begin to lose focus. By giving ourselves a 5-minute break, we easily can return to and focus on deep-thought work for another 25 minutes. This technique will make a huge impact on productivity and will also help combat procrastination. Think about it, we can endure even the most tedious dreaded task for 25 minutes, right? Once we get a little momentum going and we get immersed in the project, it becomes a lot easier. If you feel like adjusting the time a bit, go for it. I many times go 40-minutes with a 10-minute break.

If you really like this concept, the Pomodoro Technique book is a quick read. See https://francescocirillo.com/pages/pomodoro-technique.

☑ Week 18 – Do NOT Juggle Tasks Without Some Juggling Tools

Let's face it, sometimes we cannot avoid juggling emergencies. We are forced to task-switch. If you are not one of the lucky 1-2% of the population who is a "supertasker," you better have some juggling tools at your disposal to mitigate the cost of task-switching.

1. **Know Where You Left Off**

    Have a dedicated place to write down or mark where you left off when you get back, "I will do __x__." Before jumping to another task, take 15 seconds and write down this information. For instance, I draw a little hazard icon and write down where I left off/what I must do next. Sometimes I will even use a highlighter to draw more attention to it.

Finish review of restrictive covenant clause, then draft Landlord Duties.

2. **Quick Deep Breathing – Mind Check Before Commencing the New Task**

   You don't have to commit to a 15-minute mindfulness session with yourself to experience the benefits of deep breathing. You can benefit from 15-30 seconds and you don't even need to close your eyes if you don't want to. I discuss the benefits of deep breathing above, but in short, even a few deep breath starts calming the amygdala in our brain.

   Here's another method of deep breathing: Shift your breathing from your chest to your belly. Breathe in slowly (a 3-count) and say the word "Relax" on your inhale, and then exhale slowly and say the words "my Chest" (a 3-count).

   Then do your best to get oriented and then dive in to the next task.

3. **Timer to Switch Back**

   When I used to work in a kitchen, we had to juggle many things. I could have 5-10 different food items cooking at once. It was impossible to manage without timers.

   With office work, we are often doing one thing and then get pulled into a telephone call or a conversation. To help you remember to switch back, set a timer. The easiest way is to use your smartphone:

   "Hey Siri, set a timer for 15-minutes." When you start your call, be sure to politely let the caller know that you unfortunately have a hard-stop in minutes. When the 15-minutes is up, let them know that you need to wrap up.

4. **Use Checklists**

   If you constantly get pulled into multiple tasks, use checklists to minimize the possibility of missing something important. This can also make more cognitive demanding tasks less cognitively demanding because you do not have to memorize as much.

5. **Pick Tasks That Use Different Areas of the Brain**

   It is not always possible, but if you can, pick a motor task that does not compete with a cognitive task.

   For example, applying labels on envelopes (motor task) or warming up lunch in the microwave (motor task) along with a cognitive task like returning a call to your spouse (cognitive task). Be careful though, you may end up microwaving your envelopes if you try too much.

☑ Week 19 - Do NOT Carry Your Phone 24/7

Let's face it, that smartphone is a ball and chain. If you do not believe me, take a "phone fast" by leaving your phone in your car's glovebox or briefcase for a half or whole day while you are at work. Let your loved ones know how to reach you at the office in case of an emergency. You will feel liberated. It is frightening how often we look at our phones during the day. It is having a negative impact on productivity.

If for some reason, you cannot leave your phone in your briefcase, then turn off notifications on your phone and set up a VIP list for exceptions.

Also, take advantage of screen-limiting technology. For example, on your iPhone, you can use Screen Time. Go to **Settings > Screen Time**. You can view reports about how much time you have spent on your phone, within certain apps, as well as block yourself from apps during specific hours.

☑ Week 20 - Do NOT Live on Social Media 24/7

Check social media 1 or 2 times at the most during the workday (unless you are engaging in business development or marketing). In fact, think about taking a 30-day "social media fast" from all social media, and I mean all of it - Facebook, Instagram, LinkedIn, etc. - ALL OF IT. It is addictive and a huge productivity zapper. Give yourself a limit of 15-minutes a day. Set boundaries for yourself.

Social media companies design their platform using incredibly manipulative techniques to draw us in. They utilize color, monitor what we are searching for on Google to customize feeds that get your attention, and worst of all, using artificial intelligence, they know exactly what kind of posts are going to pull you in (political posts, posts about hot issues, etc.). Sometimes the best way to avoid this enticement is to stay away, especially during business hours.

☑ Week 21 —Do NOT Micro-Manage and Solve Everyone's Problems!

When you micro-manage people, you are inviting dozens of interruptions during the day. Empower the people that you pay to solve problems on their own and think for themselves. When colleagues come to you and ask what they should do, or ask how to solve a problem, the first thing out of your mouth should be:

"How do you propose that we solve this problem?"

or

"I want you to think about this and do a little research and present to me 2 or 3 possible solutions and then let's talk."

We need to get our team members to a place where they know how to problem-solve. You need to be able to delegate those problems and trust that they get resolved. Build your team members' confidence enough so they can make more decisions on their own, or, at a minimum, present the right recommendations to you.

One of my favorite books on effective delegation is *The One Minute Manager* by Kenneth Blanchard and Spencer Johnson. It is available on Amazon for less than $20.

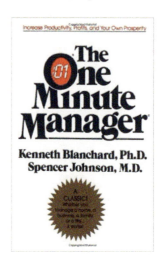

☑ Week 22 - Do NOT Create More Emails for Yourself

Don't create more emails for yourself from your responses. As an example, when trying to schedule an appointment with someone or multiple people, use applications like Doodle or Microsoft FindTime, rather than asking when everyone is available to meet. Send a quick, easy-to-create poll with FindTime or Doodle where everyone can vote on their preferred times. It holds all proposed dates on your calendar as tentative until the poll is closed and you, as the organizer, can pick the final time. Then the program sends the invitation out to all participants. It makes herding cats easy as pie, and you are not blowing up everyone's inbox with dozens of emails from all the responses.

Also, to avoid getting 10 more questions from your response, do not be vague in your emails. Always think about how to resolve the email without sparking more conversation.

Week 23 - Do NOT Process Emails All by Yourself

If you get a large volume of email every day, think about allowing a trusted assistant to help you process and respond to the email. I realize this may not be possible right away, and maybe never possible for some people, but if it is, you should strongly consider it. First and foremost, you need an assistant that you can trust with sensitive information. Second, you may need to set up an alternative email account so you can receive HR-related emails or emails from your partners, without your assistant having access to that content. Third, you need to contact your IT folks to have them give your assistant access. If using Outlook, only your Microsoft Exchange administrator would be able to give these permissions to your assistant.

☑ Week 24 - Do NOT Do Shallow Work First Thing in the Morning

Not all the time, but many times it is best to tackle deep-thought work early in the day when you are rested. Dive into deep-thought work like writing and projects early morning when you have the most energy. There is little question about it . . . our brains function better following quiet time or sleep. We also know that we can be highly productive while the rest of the world is sleeping because there are far fewer interruptions. This can be one of the most productive times of the day.

GET TRAINING & GET ORGANIZED

☑ Week 25 - Do NOT Neglect Adequate Training

Most professionals neglect training for themselves and for their team. This happens at multiple times and on multiple levels:

- **Onboarding:** We fail to have an adequate training plan for onboarding new employees. Instead, we train our people how to drive by throwing them onto the highway.

- **Ongoing Training:** Education should never stop. That is why we have "Continuing Education." Technology never stops, new situations continuously arise, and laws are constantly changing. This means we need to stay on top of those changes and adapt.

- **Software Training:** Invest in software training whenever possible. Onsite hands-on training is always the best, but it isn't always possible or within our budget. Look at tools like www.AffinityInsight.com or www.lynda.com. These solutions provide all-you-can-eat, on-demand online training for your employees, covering most of the software solutions that you use daily.

- **Process Training:** Train your people how to improve your process, not just how to perform the existing process. This means you need to explain the "why" behind the process, in addition to the process itself.

At the end of the day, when people know how to do their job and the "why" behind it, they will always be able to do things more efficiently and be able to focus on the tasks with much less stress. Education and skills bring clarity and focus. Not knowing how to do something properly can be very stressful and counterproductive.

☑ Week 26 - Do NOT Maintain a Paper File! Fight the Paper

To achieve effective distraction, time, task, and email management, we must be organized. To resolve email without delay, you must be able to find an answer quickly or know where you left off. If your documents for the Jones matter are scattered and you have to look in multiple locations, that is inevitably going to result in taking 5 times as long to answer the question and delay your response to the email until you have 30 minutes to find the answer. Here are common areas where information is typically scattered in an unorganized office:

- In a paper file called "Jones, Bill - Tax Issue"
- In someone's inbox

- In an inbox subfolder called "Jones, Bill"

- In a folder on the S drive: S:\Clients\Jones\General

- In a folder on your laptop: My Documents\Firm Stuff\Tax Issues\Jones

To be organized, we absolutely must figure out how to manage digital information in one central digital location. To make matters worse, many professionals still maintain paper files in addition to the digital file. It is an enormous waste of time and money to maintain a paper file. Paper files are nearly useless anyway in these post-Covid-19 days. Only one person can access a paper file at a time, and it is extremely time consuming and costly to store all email and other digital information in a paper file.

Bottom line: Invest in a document management system and "Fight the Paper." Check out my digital book *Fight the Paper*, available at pauljunger.com. Save emails into a central repository, as described above. Ultimately, all emails and documents for a project, case, or matter should be stored in one central location for everyone on the team to access. Tools like NetDocuments, Worldox, and iManage are perfect for this situation. Microsoft SharePoint may even be an option if it is configured properly.

Chapter 9.

APPENDIX—TDC DAILY PLANNER

The Tame the Digital Chaos (TDC) daily planner is designed to help you plan and maximize productivity on a day-to-day basis. These are undated pages that you fill out each day, as described above in Chapter 5, Task Management - Daily Planning. A bound print version of the planner is available at www.pauljunger.com, but feel free to print undated pages and fill them out on a daily basis. Here is a sample completed page. The next 2 pages contain the unfilled and undated blank form.

Date: _____

PRIORITIES

1.
2.
3.
4.
5.

GRATEFUL THOUGHTS ☺

1. _____
2. _____
3. _____

TODAY'S TIME BLOCKING

7:00 _____
8:00 _____
9:00 _____
10:00 _____
11:00 _____
12:00 _____
1:00 _____
2:00 _____
3:00 _____
4:00 _____
5:00 _____
6:00 _____
7:00 _____
8:00 _____
9:00 _____

NOTES